IN CASE OF EMERGENCY:

THE FAMILY DISASTER ORGANIZER

FROM NATURAL DISASTERS TO PANDEMICS

Everything You Need to Keep Your Family Safe

ALLISON STEWART, MPH

ADAMS MEDIA
New York London Toronto Sydney New Delhi

Adams Media
An Imprint of Simon & Schuster, Inc.
57 Littlefield Street
Avon, Massachusetts 02322

Copyright © 2020 by Simon & Schuster, Inc.

First Adams Media hardcover edition November 2020

ADAMS MEDIA and colophon are trademarks of Simon & Schuster.

For information about special discounts for bulk purchases, please contact Simon & Schuster Special Sales at 1-866-506-1949 or business@simonandschuster.com.

The Simon & Schuster Speakers Bureau can bring authors to your live event. For more information or to book an event contact the Simon & Schuster Speakers Bureau at 1-866-248-3049 or visit our website at www.simonspeakers.com.

Interior design by Colleen Cunningham
Interior images © 123RF/rana raheel abbas, Daria Chekman, Maksim Rybak, bilderriese; Getty Images/-VICTOR-, Nikiteev_Konstantin, AnnaGarmatiy, Bismillah_bd, ArnaPhoto, AVIcons

Manufactured in China

10 9 8 7 6 5 4 3 2

Library of Congress Cataloging-in-Publication Data has been applied for.

ISBN 978-1-5072-1444-2

Contains material adapted from the following titles published by Adams Media, an Imprint of Simon & Schuster, Inc.: *The Disaster Prepper's Organizer* by Walter Jacob Mullin, copyright © 2013, ISBN 978-1-4405-6526-7; *The Complete First Aid Pocket Guide* by John Furst, copyright © 2018, ISBN 978-1-5072-0888-5.

CONTENTS

PART 1
PART 2
PART 3
PART 4
PART 5
PART 6
PART 7

INTRODUCTION

It is not uncommon nowadays to read news headlines telling of emergencies on a widespread scale. *In Case of Emergency: The Family Disaster Organizer* not only shows you how to plan for an unexpected event, but also tells you what you can do to stay as safe as possible. Inside this all-in-one guide, you'll find plenty of space to record the details that matter most in your day-to-day life, from financial accounts and insurance policies to your family's blood types and medical history—there's even space to put your pets' information and a special pocket in which to store your documents. Each part covers a different aspect of emergency planning and will allow you to customize your evacuation plans and supplies in order to fit your family's specific needs.

Emergency topics covered include:

- What documents to preserve
- How to prepare for an evacuation
- When to stay in place
- How to administer basic first aid
- What to have in your survival kit

No matter what the situation, you'll find information here to help you. In addition to the major emergency hotline numbers, this organizer also includes pages where you can list the phone numbers for your local rescue agencies, your family's personal medical professionals, and other contacts you'll want to be in touch with during or right after a devastating situation. The large pocket within the book will provide you with a safe place to keep any small items or documents that you will need to take with you, including spare keys, copies of important documents, licenses, and photographs of your most valuable possessions.

Being prepared for emergencies is an act of self-empowerment. By understanding the risks that we face and responding with intelligence and readiness, you prepare yourself to stand up against the situation and make the best of it. This book will allow you to take control of your life as best as you can and give your family the opportunity to live comfortably even when your community is facing a major catastrophe. It will show you how to live in the midst of it and recover your lives when the disaster finally settles.

PART 1

The Information You'll Need

PART 1

The Information You'll Need

When dealing with a real-time emergency situation, you will probably be somewhat distracted and anxious, and understandably so. Under such stressful circumstances, locating legal and financial documents might not feel like the most pressing concern. However, if your home is devastated by a flood or fire, you and your family will need these documents to put your lives back together. Documents such as your driver's license, passport, and Social Security card provide valuable proof of identity that will be very helpful in reestablishing your life in a new place.

What to Keep in This Book

In the front plastic pocket of this book, you should include copies of each of the following vital documents, as listed by the Federal Emergency Management Agency (FEMA):

☐ Driver's licenses
☐ Birth certificates
☐ Adoption papers
☐ Social Security cards
☐ Passports
☐ Citizenship papers (such as a "green card" or naturalization documents)
☐ Marriage license
☐ Divorce decrees
☐ Child custody papers
☐ Current military ID
☐ Military discharge (DD Form 214)
☐ Medical and vaccination records for pets along with current photos and ID chip numbers in case you are separated

All of these documents should be contained in a sealable plastic bag so they're protected from water damage.

For other documents, including insurance policies (homeowners, renters, flood, earthquake, auto, life, health, disability, long-term care, etc.), have at least the policy number and insurance company contact information for each type of coverage. I recommend readers save these files on the cloud and on a thumb drive. The thumb drive should go inside a sealable plastic bag to ensure its safety before it goes into the plastic pocket in the book.

The secondary pocket in the back of the book can be used for extras like paper maps, pamphlets from FEMA or any other organization that are relevant during a crisis (mailers, instructions, documents you print out with new instructions), and anything else that you grab on your way out the door, or that you will receive during evacuation.

As you read this list, you might think of more documents or items that are important to you. To be as prepared as possible, think about what kinds of things you'd need in order to continue living your life after an emergency. The original copies should be kept in a safe-deposit box in a bank; another copy could be given to family members who don't live with you; and a third copy should be filed away in a floodproof/fireproof box in your home office. You can keep a key to the safe-deposit box in the pocket of this book. If some of these documents can be accessed electronically, you might also opt to protect them with a password and store them on an external drive or on a secure cloud-based service.

An additional way to protect your family's documents is to record all of their important ID numbers in this book. This way, even if the documents are lost, you will have the numbers needed to access the information and replace the documents.

Your Family's Important Documents

Here is a section for document ID numbers. Be sure to fill this out completely for each member of your family.

Your Family's Important Documents

Family Member #1

Name: _____

Passport number: _____

Social Security number: _____

Driver's license number: _____

Immigration number (if applicable): _____

Other: _____

Other: _____

Family Member #2

Name: _____

Passport number: _____

Social Security number: _____

Driver's license number: _____

Immigration number (if applicable): _____

Other: _____

Other: _____

Family Member #3

Name: _____

Passport number: _____

Social Security number: _____

Driver's license number: _____

Immigration number (if applicable): _____

Other: _____

Other: _____

Family Member #4

Name: _____

Passport number: _____

Social Security number: _____

Driver's license number: _____

Immigration number (if applicable): _____

Other: _____

Other: _____

Family Member #5

Name: _____

Passport number: _____

Social Security number: _____

Driver's license number: _____

Immigration number (if applicable): _____

Other: _____

Other: _____

Family Member #6

Name: _____

Passport number: _____

Social Security number: _____

Driver's license number: _____

Immigration number (if applicable): _____

Other: _____

Other: _____

Your Family's Medical Information

Complete medical information contains your current conditions, medications, vaccinations, and a family medical history. Traditionally, a family medical history is a complete record of health information from three generations of relatives. This assists doctors in understanding any genetic predispositions your family might have to illnesses such as heart disease, high blood pressure, stroke, certain types of cancer, and diabetes. Knowing each family's history of hospitalizations, surgeries, and addictions may also help first responders determine how best to proceed.

For the purposes of an emergency, it is unlikely that you will need medical information for three generations of family members. Instead, list any known family history for the members of your household. It may be useful to ask your parents or elder family members about your family's history.

PART 1

Family Member #1

Name: _____

Date of birth: _____/_____/_____

Family member's health insurance company: _____

Group number: _____

ID number: _____

Blood Type

☐ A+ ☐ B+ ☐ O+ ☐ AB+

☐ A- ☐ B- ☐ O- ☐ AB-

Personal Medical History

Please check all that apply to you:

☐ Anemia
☐ Arthritis
☐ Asthma
☐ Cancer
☐ Blood disease or clotting disorder
☐ COPD
☐ Other cardiac issues
☐ Congestive heart failure
☐ Crohn's disease
☐ Thyroid issues
☐ Cardiac arrhythmia
☐ Syncope (fainting)
☐ Dental fillings
☐ Psychiatric condition
☐ Depression
☐ Diabetes
☐ Lung disease
☐ Endocrine issues
☐ Epilepsy
☐ GERD
☐ Vision issues

☐ Hepatitis
☐ Tuberculosis
☐ Blood transfusion
☐ Spina bifida
☐ Gum disease
☐ Hearing issues
☐ HIV/AIDS
☐ Hypertension
☐ Kidney disease
☐ Myocardial infarction
☐ Peptic ulcer
☐ Pregnancy
☐ Stroke
☐ Ulcerative colitis
☐ Generalized anxiety
☐ Chemotherapy
☐ Physical disability
☐ Infective endocarditis
☐ Cystic fibrosis
☐ Other: _____
☐ Other: _____

Your Family's Medical Information

Family Member #1—continued

Please list previous surgeries and hospitalizations with dates:

_____

_____

_____

Please list any environmental, pharmaceutical, or food allergies:

_____

_____

_____

Please list any medications (including supplements) with dose and frequency:

_____

_____

_____

Vaccination History [Date]:

Tdap/DTaP: _____

Influenza: _____

Meningococcal: _____

Pneumococcal: _____

MMR: _____

Hepatitis B: _____

Rotavirus: _____

Varicella: _____

Hib: _____

Polio: _____

Hepatitis A; Yellow Fever: _____

HPV: _____

Shingles: _____

Other: _____

Healthcare Providers [Specialty/Name/Phone Number]:

Primary care provider: _____

Dentist: _____

Local hospital: _____

Other: _____

Family Member #2

Name: _____

Date of birth: ____/____/____

Family member's health insurance company: _____

Group number: _____

ID number: _____

Blood Type

☐ A+   ☐ B+   ☐ O+   ☐ AB+

☐ A-   ☐ B-   ☐ O-   ☐ AB-

Personal Medical History

Please check all that apply to you:

☐ Anemia
☐ Arthritis
☐ Asthma
☐ Cancer
☐ Blood disease or clotting disorder
☐ COPD
☐ Other cardiac issues
☐ Congestive heart failure
☐ Crohn's disease
☐ Thyroid issues
☐ Cardiac arrhythmia
☐ Syncope (fainting)
☐ Dental fillings
☐ Psychiatric condition
☐ Depression
☐ Diabetes
☐ Lung disease
☐ Endocrine issues
☐ Epilepsy
☐ GERD
☐ Vision issues

☐ Hepatitis
☐ Tuberculosis
☐ Blood transfusion
☐ Spina bifida
☐ Gum disease
☐ Hearing issues
☐ HIV/AIDS
☐ Hypertension
☐ Kidney disease
☐ Myocardial infarction
☐ Peptic ulcer
☐ Pregnancy
☐ Stroke
☐ Ulcerative colitis
☐ Generalized anxiety
☐ Chemotherapy
☐ Physical disability
☐ Infective endocarditis
☐ Cystic fibrosis
☐ Other: _____
☐ Other: _____

Your Family's Medical Information

Family Member #2—continued

Please list previous surgeries and hospitalizations with dates:

_____

_____

_____

Please list any environmental, pharmaceutical, or food allergies:

_____

_____

_____

Please list any medications (including supplements) with dose and frequency:

_____

_____

_____

Vaccination History [Date]:

Tdap/DTaP: _____ Varicella: _____

Influenza: _____ Hib: _____

Meningococcal: _____ Polio: _____

Pneumococcal: _____ Hepatitis A; Yellow Fever: _____

MMR: _____ HPV: _____

Hepatitis B: _____ Shingles: _____

Rotavirus: _____ Other: _____

Healthcare Providers [Specialty / Name / Phone Number]:

Primary care provider: _____

Dentist: _____

Local hospital: _____

Other: _____

PART 1

Family Member #3

Name: _____

Date of birth: _____/_____/_____

Family member's health insurance company: _____

Group number: _____

ID number: _____

Blood Type

☐ A+ ☐ B+ ☐ O+ ☐ AB+

☐ A- ☐ B- ☐ O- ☐ AB-

Personal Medical History

Please check all that apply to you:

☐ Anemia

☐ Arthritis

☐ Asthma

☐ Cancer

☐ Blood disease or clotting disorder

☐ COPD

☐ Other cardiac issues

☐ Congestive heart failure

☐ Crohn's disease

☐ Thyroid issues

☐ Cardiac arrhythmia

☐ Syncope (fainting)

☐ Dental fillings

☐ Psychiatric condition

☐ Depression

☐ Diabetes

☐ Lung disease

☐ Endocrine issues

☐ Epilepsy

☐ GERD

☐ Vision issues

☐ Hepatitis

☐ Tuberculosis

☐ Blood transfusion

☐ Spina bifida

☐ Gum disease

☐ Hearing issues

☐ HIV/AIDS

☐ Hypertension

☐ Kidney disease

☐ Myocardial infarction

☐ Peptic ulcer

☐ Pregnancy

☐ Stroke

☐ Ulcerative colitis

☐ Generalized anxiety

☐ Chemotherapy

☐ Physical disability

☐ Infective endocarditis

☐ Cystic fibrosis

☐ Other: _____

☐ Other: _____

Your Family's Medical Information

Family Member #3—continued

Please list previous surgeries and hospitalizations with dates:

_____

_____

_____

Please list any environmental, pharmaceutical, or food allergies:

_____

_____

_____

Please list any medications (including supplements) with dose and frequency:

_____

_____

_____

Vaccination History [Date]:

Tdap/DTaP: _____   Varicella: _____

Influenza: _____   Hib: _____

Meningococcal: _____   Polio: _____

Pneumococcal: _____   Hepatitis A; Yellow Fever: _____

MMR: _____   HPV: _____

Hepatitis B: _____   Shingles: _____

Rotavirus: _____   Other: _____

Healthcare Providers [Specialty / Name / Phone Number]:

Primary care provider: _____

Dentist: _____

Local hospital: _____

Other: _____

PART 1

Family Member #4

Name: _____

Date of birth: ____/____/____

Family member's health insurance company: _____

Group number: _____

ID number: _____

Blood Type

☐ A+   ☐ B+   ☐ O+   ☐ AB+

☐ A-   ☐ B-   ☐ O-   ☐ AB-

Personal Medical History

Please check all that apply to you:

☐ Anemia   ☐ Hepatitis

☐ Arthritis   ☐ Tuberculosis

☐ Asthma   ☐ Blood transfusion

☐ Cancer   ☐ Spina bifida

☐ Blood disease or clotting disorder   ☐ Gum disease

☐ COPD   ☐ Hearing issues

☐ Other cardiac issues   ☐ HIV/AIDS

☐ Congestive heart failure   ☐ Hypertension

☐ Crohn's disease   ☐ Kidney disease

☐ Thyroid issues   ☐ Myocardial infarction

☐ Cardiac arrhythmia   ☐ Peptic ulcer

☐ Syncope (fainting)   ☐ Pregnancy

☐ Dental fillings   ☐ Stroke

☐ Psychiatric condition   ☐ Ulcerative colitis

☐ Depression   ☐ Generalized anxiety

☐ Diabetes   ☐ Chemotherapy

☐ Lung disease   ☐ Physical disability

☐ Endocrine issues   ☐ Infective endocarditis

☐ Epilepsy   ☐ Cystic fibrosis

☐ GERD   ☐ Other: _____

☐ Vision issues   ☐ Other: _____

Your Family's Medical Information

PART 1

Family Member #4—continued

Please list previous surgeries and hospitalizations with dates:

_____

_____

_____

Please list any environmental, pharmaceutical, or food allergies:

_____

_____

_____

Please list any medications (including supplements) with dose and frequency:

_____

_____

_____

Vaccination History [Date]:

Tdap/DTaP: _____   Varicella: _____

Influenza: _____   Hib: _____

Meningococcal: _____   Polio: _____

Pneumococcal: _____   Hepatitis A; Yellow Fever: _____

MMR: _____   HPV: _____

Hepatitis B: _____   Shingles: _____

Rotavirus: _____   Other: _____

Healthcare Providers [Specialty / Name / Phone Number]:

Primary care provider: _____

Dentist: _____

Local hospital: _____

Other: _____

PART 1

Family Member #5

Name: _____

Date of birth: _____/_____/_____

Family member's health insurance company: _____

Group number: _____

ID number: _____

Blood Type

☐ A+   ☐ B+   ☐ O+   ☐ AB+

☐ A-   ☐ B-   ☐ O-   ☐ AB-

Personal Medical History

Please check all that apply to you:

☐ Anemia   ☐ Hepatitis
☐ Arthritis   ☐ Tuberculosis
☐ Asthma   ☐ Blood transfusion
☐ Cancer   ☐ Spina bifida
☐ Blood disease or clotting disorder   ☐ Gum disease
☐ COPD   ☐ Hearing issues
☐ Other cardiac issues   ☐ HIV/AIDS
☐ Congestive heart failure   ☐ Hypertension
☐ Crohn's disease   ☐ Kidney disease
☐ Thyroid issues   ☐ Myocardial infarction
☐ Cardiac arrhythmia   ☐ Peptic ulcer
☐ Syncope (fainting)   ☐ Pregnancy
☐ Dental fillings   ☐ Stroke
☐ Psychiatric condition   ☐ Ulcerative colitis
☐ Depression   ☐ Generalized anxiety
☐ Diabetes   ☐ Chemotherapy
☐ Lung disease   ☐ Physical disability
☐ Endocrine issues   ☐ Infective endocarditis
☐ Epilepsy   ☐ Cystic fibrosis
☐ GERD   ☐ Other: _____
☐ Vision issues   ☐ Other: _____

Your Family's Medical Information

Family Member #5—continued

Please list previous surgeries and hospitalizations with dates:

_____

_____

_____

Please list any environmental, pharmaceutical, or food allergies:

_____

_____

_____

Please list any medications (including supplements) with dose and frequency:

_____

_____

_____

Vaccination History [Date]:

Tdap/DTaP: _____   Varicella: _____

Influenza: _____   Hib: _____

Meningococcal: _____   Polio: _____

Pneumococcal: _____   Hepatitis A; Yellow Fever: _____

MMR: _____   HPV: _____

Hepatitis B: _____   Shingles: _____

Rotavirus: _____   Other: _____

Healthcare Providers [Specialty/Name/Phone Number]:

Primary care provider: _____

Dentist: _____

Local hospital: _____

Other: _____

PART 1

Family Member #6

Name: _____

Date of birth: _____/_____/_____

Family member's health insurance company: _____

Group number: _____

ID number: _____

Blood Type

- ☐ A+
- ☐ A-
- ☐ B+
- ☐ B-
- ☐ O+
- ☐ O-
- ☐ AB+
- ☐ AB-

Personal Medical History

Please check all that apply to you:

- ☐ Anemia
- ☐ Arthritis
- ☐ Asthma
- ☐ Cancer
- ☐ Blood disease or clotting disorder
- ☐ COPD
- ☐ Other cardiac issues
- ☐ Congestive heart failure
- ☐ Crohn's disease
- ☐ Thyroid issues
- ☐ Cardiac arrhythmia
- ☐ Syncope (fainting)
- ☐ Dental fillings
- ☐ Psychiatric condition
- ☐ Depression
- ☐ Diabetes
- ☐ Lung disease
- ☐ Endocrine issues
- ☐ Epilepsy
- ☐ GERD
- ☐ Vision issues

- ☐ Hepatitis
- ☐ Tuberculosis
- ☐ Blood transfusion
- ☐ Spina bifida
- ☐ Gum disease
- ☐ Hearing issues
- ☐ HIV/AIDS
- ☐ Hypertension
- ☐ Kidney disease
- ☐ Myocardial infarction
- ☐ Peptic ulcer
- ☐ Pregnancy
- ☐ Stroke
- ☐ Ulcerative colitis
- ☐ Generalized anxiety
- ☐ Chemotherapy
- ☐ Physical disability
- ☐ Infective endocarditis
- ☐ Cystic fibrosis
- ☐ Other: _____
- ☐ Other: _____

Your Family's Medical Information

Family Member #6—continued

Please list previous surgeries and hospitalizations with dates:

_____

_____

_____

Please list any environmental, pharmaceutical, or food allergies:

_____

_____

_____

Please list any medications (including supplements) with dose and frequency:

_____

_____

_____

Vaccination History [Date]:

Tdap/DTaP: _____   Varicella: _____

Influenza: _____   Hib: _____

Meningococcal: _____   Polio: _____

Pneumococcal: _____   Hepatitis A; Yellow Fever: _____

MMR: _____   HPV: _____

Hepatitis B: _____   Shingles: _____

Rotavirus: _____   Other: _____

Healthcare Providers [Specialty / Name / Phone Number]:

Primary care provider: _____

Dentist: _____

Local hospital: _____

Other: _____

Pets

For many of us, our pets are members of the family, and when an emergency happens, we want to make sure they are safe. Like humans, pets may be afraid or anxious during a natural disaster, fire, or terrorist attack. Unlike humans, however, pets do not understand the need to evacuate during an emergency and may be skittish in unfamiliar surroundings. As the owner, you will need to act on your pet's behalf to keep the animal safe and as calm as possible. As with most of the situations you may encounter during an emergency, preplanning ways to provide for your pet is the best way to be calm and confident in the moment. According to the *Ready* website, www.ready.gov, run by the US Federal Emergency Management Agency (FEMA), what is best for you and your family is usually also best for your pets. You should *not* leave your pets behind during an emergency evacuation; in most cases, abandoned pets are not able to survive on their own.

✦ Microchipping Your Pet

During the chaos of an emergency situation, one of the biggest concerns for pet owners is losing track of or becoming separated from their pet. For this reason, it is crucial to have various identification methods in place in the event of a separation.

The most common form of pet identification is a collar with visible ID tags. In addition to pet licensing and rabies shot information, these tags should include your pet's name, your full name and address, and all relevant contact information. You should also include the name and phone number of your pet's veterinarian, in case you can't be reached. If your pet has been microchipped, you should also have a tag for the collar that includes the chip ID number and registry phone number.

ID tags are the standard form of pet identification and significantly increase your chances of being reunited with your pet. However, during an emergency, it is possible that your pet's collar might come off due to your pet's panicked movements, weather damage, or other extreme conditions. This is why it is so useful to have your pet microchipped. According to the Humane Society of the United States, microchips are tiny transponders, roughly the size of a grain of rice, which use radio frequency waves to convey information about your pet. They are implanted just under your pet's skin, usually between the shoulder blades.

Each pet's microchip usually consists of a registration number, as well as the phone number of the registry for the specific brand of chip. This information can be accessed and displayed at animal shelters and veterinary clinics through a handheld scanner. The veterinary clinic or animal shelter can then call the registry to get your name and phone number.

You can get your pet microchipped at many veterinary offices and some animal shelters for a small fee. According to the Humane Society of the United States, the procedure is done with a large-bore needle and does not require anesthesia. Microchips are designed to last for around twenty-five years.

It is very important to remember that just having the chip is *not* enough—it is essential that you fill out the paperwork that comes with the chip and send it to the registry, or fill out the form online if that is an option. Some microchip companies charge a onetime registration fee, while others charge an annual fee. Remember to stay up-to-date on registration payments so your pet will remain registered. Likewise, if you should move or change your contact information, you need to contact the microchip company to update your information in the registry. Otherwise, the microchip will not be effective in helping reunite you with your pet. You should also make sure you have a tag for your pet's collar with the microchip number and registry phone number on it.

FEMA also recommends taking a picture of you and your pet together. In the event of an emergency in which you and your pet are separated, this photo will help you establish ownership and allow others to help you identify your pet.

Your Pet's Information

Use this section to provide detailed identifying information about each of your pets, including relevant ID numbers and distinguishing characteristics.

Pet #1

Name: _____

Species: _____

Breed: _____

Year of birth: _____

Sex: ☐ Male   ☐ Female   Spayed/neutered?   ☐ Yes   ☐ No

Identifiers

Color: _____

Describe pet (markings, etc.): _____

What color is your pet's collar?_____

Is your pet microchipped?   ☐ Yes   ☐ No   Microchip number: _____

Microchip registry name and phone number: _____

Medical History

List all vaccines your pet is currently up-to-date on:

_____

_____

List any health conditions this pet has:

_____

_____

What medications does your pet take? Include dosage/color of pill.

_____

_____

_____

_____

Name and phone number of veterinarian:

_____

_____

Your Pet's Information

Pet #2

Name: _____

Species: _____

Breed: _____

Year of birth: _____

Sex: ☐ Male   ☐ Female   Spayed/neutered?   ☐ Yes   ☐ No

Identifiers

Color: _____

Describe pet (markings, etc.): _____

What color is your pet's collar?_____

Is your pet microchipped?   ☐ Yes   ☐ No   Microchip number: _____

Microchip registry name and phone number: _____

Medical History

List all vaccines your pet is currently up-to-date on:

_____

_____

List any health conditions this pet has:

_____

_____

What medications does your pet take? Include dosage/color of pill:

_____

_____

_____

_____

Name and phone number of veterinarian:

_____

_____

Pet #3

Name: _____

Species: _____

Breed: _____

Year of birth: _____

Sex: ☐ Male ☐ Female   Spayed/neutered? ☐ Yes ☐ No

Identifiers

Color: _____

Describe pet (markings, etc.): _____

What color is your pet's collar?_____

Is your pet microchipped? ☐ Yes ☐ No   Microchip number: _____

Microchip registry name and phone number: _____

Medical History

List all vaccines your pet is currently up-to-date on:

_____

_____

List any health conditions this pet has:

_____

_____

What medications does your pet take? Include dosage/color of pill:

_____

_____

_____

_____

Name and phone number of veterinarian:

_____

_____

Your Pet's Information

Pet #4

Name: _____

Species: _____

Breed: _____

Year of birth: _____

Sex: ☐ Male   ☐ Female   Spayed/neutered?   ☐ Yes   ☐ No

Identifiers

Color: _____

Describe pet (markings, etc.): _____

What color is your pet's collar?_____

Is your pet microchipped?   ☐ Yes   ☐ No   Microchip number: _____

Microchip registry name and phone number: _____

Medical History

List all vaccines your pet is currently up-to-date on:

_____

_____

List any health conditions this pet has:

_____

_____

What medications does your pet take? Include dosage/color of pill:

_____

_____

_____

_____

Name and phone number of veterinarian:

_____

_____

Pet #5

Name: _____

Species: _____

Breed: _____

Year of birth: _____

Sex: ☐ Male ☐ Female Spayed/neutered? ☐ Yes ☐ No

Identifiers

Color: _____

Describe pet (markings, etc.): _____

What color is your pet's collar?_____

Is your pet microchipped? ☐ Yes ☐ No   Microchip number: _____

Microchip registry name and phone number: _____

Medical History

List all vaccines your pet is currently up-to-date on:

_____

_____

List any health conditions this pet has:

_____

_____

What medications does your pet take? Include dosage/color of pill:

_____

_____

_____

_____

Name and phone number of veterinarian:

_____

_____

Your Pet's Information

Pet #6

Name: _____

Species: _____

Breed: _____

Year of birth: _____

Sex: □ Male   □ Female   Spayed/neutered?   □ Yes   □ No

Identifiers

Color: _____

Describe pet (markings, etc.): _____

What color is your pet's collar?_____

Is your pet microchipped?   □ Yes   □ No   Microchip number: _____

Microchip registry name and phone number: _____

Medical History

List all vaccines your pet is currently up-to-date on:

_____

_____

List any health conditions this pet has:

_____

_____

What medications does your pet take? Include dosage/color of pill:

_____

_____

_____

_____

Name and phone number of veterinarian:

_____

_____

National Contacts

Humane Society of the United States:
1-202-452-1100 (nonemergency number)

American Society for the Prevention of Cruelty to Animals:
1-888-666-2279 (nonemergency number)

Other Contacts

Local SPCA/humane society phone number:

_____

Nearby veterinary hospital:

_____

Out-of-area veterinary hospital:

_____

Name, phone number of pet care buddy:

_____

Lodging

Pet-friendly hotel/motel #1:

_____

Pet-friendly hotel/motel #2:

_____

Pet-friendly hotel/motel #3:

_____

Kennel/other lodging:

_____

_____

What to Keep with This Guide

PART 1

In the next few parts, you'll learn more about how to prepare for disasters, but before you do, it's a good idea to get all your documents organized and stored in the book's pocket. The following is a checklist of the documents, photographs, and other items you need to take with you during an emergency.

Legal/Identifying Documents (Copies)

- ☐ Birth certificates
- ☐ Marriage certificates
- ☐ Divorce decrees
- ☐ Child custody/adoption documentation
- ☐ Immigration documentation (citizenship papers or naturalization documents)
- ☐ Wills (including trusts, living wills, advance directives)
- ☐ Passports
- ☐ Social Security cards
- ☐ Driver's licenses
- ☐ Medical records (including healthcare action plans, if applicable) and vaccination documents
- ☐ Financial records (copy)
- ☐ Health insurance cards/papers
- ☐ Military records
- ☐ Personal insurance records

Property Documents/Items

- ☐ Title/deed of house (copy)
- ☐ Mortgage papers/rental agreement (copy)
- ☐ Mortgage discharge document
- ☐ Key to safe-deposit box
- ☐ Spare house key
- ☐ External drive/cloud service information containing documents/photos
- ☐ Homeowners insurance paperwork (copy)
- ☐ Tax records (copy)
- ☐ Vehicle titles (copy)
- ☐ Photographs of household possessions
- ☐ Receipts for expensive items
- ☐ Cash
- ☐ Credit card

What to Keep with This Guide

PART 1

Evacuation/Vehicle Items

☐ Evacuation/storm surge maps
☐ Copy of vehicle insurance/registration
☐ Copy of roadside assistance card

Pet-Related Items

☐ Photograph of you and pet
☐ Pet license/registration (copy)
☐ Pet adoption paperwork
☐ Pet first aid book/pamphlet
☐ Pet medical records and vaccination papers (copy)
☐ Pet microchip number

PART 2

When to Stay Put

PART 2

PART 2

When to Stay Put

During some emergencies, the best course of action in order to remain safe is to shelter in place. Certain disasters may come on suddenly, requiring you to be ready to handle these situations where you live—and many outbreaks necessitate isolation and quarantine. For this reason, it is helpful to keep a stock of necessary supplies at home, including materials to safeguard your home. Knowing that you have the tools to protect yourself and your loved ones in an emergency can offer peace of mind. This part will give you an overview of the types of disasters and outbreaks that may require you to shelter at home.

Preparing for a Disaster at Home

The most important thing you can do to prepare for a natural or chemical disaster is to develop a plan of action and practice drills with your family. Many disasters require evacuation, but some come on so quickly that sheltering in place is the safer choice. You should always follow official guidance on which course of action is appropriate for your situation. Outlined here are some disaster scenarios that may require sheltering in place and the ways you can prepare for them.

+ Sheltering During a Tornado

Like most severe weather events, tornadoes are subject to a well-developed early warning system. It's important to learn about your tornado warning system—most areas that are prone to tornadoes have a siren system. Tornado watches and warnings are also issued locally; tornado watches are for those occasions when weather conditions indicate that tornadoes could form, and warnings are issued when a tornado is sighted or indicated by radar. During inclement weather, stay tuned to your local radio or TV stations or a National Oceanic and Atmospheric Administration (NOAA) weather radio.

When taking shelter from a tornado, the key rule is to pick a place away from windows. The safest area in a home is the interior of a basement, but if your home doesn't have a basement, use an inside room, preferably with no windows, on the lowest level of the house. For added protection for your entire body, get under a heavy table or desk, and cover your body with a blanket or sleeping bag and protect your head. Do not stay in a mobile home during a tornado; go to the nearest building with a tornado shelter space. Do not try to outrun a tornado in a vehicle; if there isn't time to make it to the nearest shelter, lie flat in a ditch, ravine, or culvert and shield your head.

✦ Sheltering During an Earthquake

Surviving an earthquake and reducing its impact requires planning and practice by you and your family. If you live in an earthquake-prone area, you can gather and keep supplies months in advance. One of the most important preparedness steps for an earthquake is to inspect your home for hazards. During an earthquake or its aftershocks, anything can move, break, or fall. You should check all the rooms in your house for the following hazards and secure them appropriately:

☐ Unanchored furniture or appliances or heavy items that may fall over (bookcases, cabinets, refrigerators, TVs, water heaters, stands, etc.)
☐ Windows or other glass breakables
☐ Areas that could become blocked by falling debris
☐ Hanging or overhead items (ceiling fans, mirrors, pictures, etc.)
☐ Hazardous materials (poisons, solvents, cleaning supplies, etc.)

Make sure to locate the utility shutoffs in your home: electrical, water, and gas.

The Centers for Disease Control and Prevention (CDC) advises you to drop, cover, and hold on during an earthquake: *Drop* down onto your hands and knees, *cover* your head and neck (but preferably your entire body) under a sturdy desk or table, and *hold on* to your shelter (the desk or table) until the shaking stops. Do not stand in a doorway, as doorways in modern homes are not any more stable than any other part of the home. If you (or a member of your household) have limited mobility, you should try to sit or remain seated, lock your wheels (if applicable), and protect your head and neck from falling debris with a pillow, a large book, or your arms. It's important to practice these techniques in earthquake drills with your whole family.

Once the earthquake is over, follow your family's home evacuation plan to get clear of damaged buildings or structures.

✦ Sheltering During a Radiological Event

Radiation emergencies can be caused by a nuclear power plant explosion or accident or a dirty bomb. In the event of a radiation emergency, the CDC stresses that it's important to get inside quickly, stay inside, and stay tuned. If you are in an area directly affected by a radiation emergency, you may need to decontaminate yourself before entering your home. In order to self-decontaminate, take off (and bag) your outer layer of clothing; protecting any cuts, wash yourself off with soap and water preferably with a shower (but do not use conditioner in your hair); and put on clean clothes. Pets that were outside will need to be decontaminated as well—wash them with soap and water while wearing gloves and a face mask, making sure to protect any cuts on you or your pet. Remember to wash your face and hands afterward. After entering your home, close and lock all windows and doors. Shelter in the basement or an interior part of the home; stay as far away from exterior walls and the roof as you can. If possible, turn off fans and HVAC units, and close fireplace dampers. Stay tuned for announcements from emergency response officials for updated instructions.

✦ Sheltering During a Chemical Spill or Other Chemical Hazard

Chemical emergencies happen when toxic substances are released into a community, sometimes necessitating the issue of shelter-in-place orders by local officials. Chemical emergencies can also necessitate "do not use" water orders if the chemical leaks into municipal or groundwater sources. You should not shelter in vehicles as they are not airtight enough to protect you from chemical releases. Unlike other natural disasters, the recommended area for sheltering in place for a chemical emergency is the highest floor of a residence, as this can protect you from gaseous vapors that sink (they are heavier than air). Choose an interior room with a running water source and without windows, if possible.

Every chemical emergency situation is different, so it's important to follow any special instructions that local emergency coordinators might have for your area, but generally, the following steps should be taken:

- ☐ Get family members (including pets) inside as quickly as possible.
- ☐ If you have time, shut and lock all doors and windows; doing so may provide a tighter seal. Turn off any fans and HVAC units and close any fireplace dampers.
- ☐ Go into the shelter-in-place room and close the door.
- ☐ Turn on a radio and keep a telephone close by, but only use the phone for emergencies.
- ☐ Use plastic sheeting and duct tape to seal the room. Use duct tape over any vents in the room and use it to seal electrical outlets and any other openings.
- ☐ Listen to the radio for updates on when it's safe to leave the shelter, and follow the guidance of the emergency response coordinators for next steps.

✦ Sheltering During a Volcanic Eruption

Depending on your location, sheltering in place during a volcanic eruption may be the recommended course of action. However, it's imperative that you follow the advice of local officials: If they say to evacuate, evacuate early. If evacuation is not recommended by local officials, then you can stay safe indoors by doing the following things:

- ☐ Close all windows, doors, and fireplace dampers.
- ☐ Turn off all fans and HVAC units.
- ☐ Make sure to bring pets and livestock into closed shelters as well.
- ☐ If ashfall is a concern, wear goggles and long pants and long-sleeved shirts, and don an N95 respirator.

After a volcanic eruption, follow the advice of local officials. Listen to your local news for updates on air quality (and when it's safe to go outdoors), water quality, and road conditions.

✚ Sheltering During an Outbreak

Outbreaks can be caused by many infectious disease agents, including viruses, bacteria, and parasites. Each type of infectious agent can be transmitted from a natural reservoir to a susceptible host in different ways that are classified as the following:

DIRECT:

- Direct contact (e.g., touching, kissing, sexual contact)
- Droplet spread (large droplets from coughing or sneezing that travel up to 6 feet and fall to a surface)

INDIRECT:

- Airborne (microscopic particles that can stay suspended in the air for a period of time)
- Vehicle-borne (the transferring of infectious agents from the surface of an inanimate object or from food and water)
- Vector-borne (the transferring of infectious agents from an insect or animal, known as a "vector")

Depending on the type of outbreak, protective measures—including pharmaceutical and nonpharmaceutical interventions (NPIs)—can be taken at the personal and community level. Contingent on the type of disease threat, there may be a vaccine or prophylactic treatment available, and it's incredibly important to stay up-to-date on all routine vaccinations, including a yearly flu shot. Many infections that cause outbreaks will look similar to other infections, like the flu, so remaining protected by vaccination against those other infectious disease threats is the most important planning that you can do.

If a new infectious disease threat emerges that spreads rapidly from person to person worldwide, causing a pandemic, a vaccine or prophylactic therapy may not be immediately available. In those circumstances, because the disease is new, the human population has little or no immunity against it, which allows the infection to spread quickly. NPIs—also known as community mitigation strategies—are actions that people and communities can take to help slow the spread of illnesses during these types of outbreaks and pandemics. NPIs are among the best ways of controlling pandemics when pharmaceutical interventions are not yet available.

This makes planning and working together as a community even more important. Though difficult to plan and carry out, community NPIs (such as social distancing and temporary school closures) can help everyone protect the health of the community as a whole. To ensure the greatest impact, the CDC recommends that communities incorporate a combination of personal NPIs, community NPIs, and environmental NPIs into their pandemic plans.

✚ Personal NPIs

Many personal NPIs are recommended at all times, regardless of whether there is an outbreak or pandemic. These NPIs include:

- Staying home when sick.
- Covering coughs and sneezes appropriately (using a tissue or the inside of your elbow, not your hand).
- Washing hands often (especially after using the restroom and before eating) with soap and water for at least twenty seconds (see Guide to Handwashing in this part and Handwashing to Protect Yourself from Infection in the **APPENDIX**). Using at least a 60 percent alcohol-based hand sanitizer if soap and water are not available.
- Routinely cleaning frequently used surfaces.

During an outbreak or pandemic, additional personal NPIs may be recommended by your local health department or the CDC. These may include not touching your face, a recommended degree of social distancing, the use of a face mask, washing or sanitizing hands before entering public spaces, or other additional measures, depending on the type of disease.

GUIDE TO HANDWASHING:

1. Wet hands with clean running water.
2. Apply enough soap to cover all surfaces of your hands.
3. Rub hands palm to palm to lather.
4. Rub the top of your left hand with your right hand, and interlace the fingers; then switch to the other hand.
5. Rub your hands palm to palm with your fingers interlaced.
6. Rub the backs of your fingers against the opposing palm, then switch; rub the backs of your hands together.
7. Hold your right thumb in your left fist and rotate, then switch.
8. Rub your nails/the tips of your fingers against the opposite palm (this cleans under your nails), then switch.
9. Place your right hand over your left wrist and scrub by twisting your hand, then switch.
10. After scrubbing your hands for at least twenty seconds, rinse.
11. Dry hands thoroughly with a disposable towel.
12. Use the towel to turn off the faucet.

Your hands are now clean.

✦ Community NPIs

During an outbreak or a pandemic, community or environmental NPIs may be instituted on an organizational, local, state, or national level. It's incredibly important to follow the recommendations or statutes laid out by local or national officials during a time of pandemic or outbreak. Some community-based NPIs you might see are:

- The implementation of telework arrangements by organizations whenever possible.
- The cancellation of gatherings over a certain amount of people, which includes gatherings in bars, restaurants, theaters, libraries, etc.
- The closing of schools and universities.
- Limits on visitors to high-risk facilities such as nursing homes, daycares, or hospitals.

- Local or national lockdown orders and freedom of movement limitations (such as curfews and nonessential travel directives).
- Legal quarantine or isolation orders (typically quarantines are used to isolate and limit movement of people who are apparently well—including those who might have been exposed to the disease—and isolation is used to separate ill people from healthy).

Community NPIs can be very disruptive and can feel very stressful, but it's important to stay calm and heed the advice of scientists, doctors, and officials during a time of novel disease threats. Doing so will help save lives.

During large outbreaks and pandemics, the CDC usually sets up a dedicated website to get information quickly to healthcare professionals and to the public. Make sure to check www.cdc.gov for more information during a pandemic. Pandemic information can also be found on the World Health Organization (WHO) website at www.who.int.

Creating a Two-Week Survival Kit

The most likely emergency that will result in an extended period of home-based sheltering is an outbreak or pandemic. Most other emergencies will only involve sheltering for a time before evacuating, and you can utilize your seventy-two-hour kit (see **PART 3**). For an outbreak or pandemic situation, however, you may have to quarantine or isolate for a longer period, and there may be a run on necessary supplies at local stores, as there might be some warning ahead of time. For this reason, it's helpful to maintain at least two weeks of supplies on hand at all times—as well as the supplies in your seventy-two-hour kit.

During a pandemic, interruptions to essential services are generally unlikely but could occur. It should be noted, however, that in the case of an outbreak or pandemic, *it's very important to not hoard supplies*. Get enough to last two weeks, but leave some for your fellow community members.

The following checklist includes suggestions that you may want to consider.

✦ Food and Water

Similar to your seventy-two-hour supply, you will need enough food and water for your entire family. Since vital service disruptions aren't likely, having only seventy-two hours of water on hand will be sufficient for most emergencies. However, it's important to stock food for a couple of weeks—a mix of shelf-stable, frozen, and fresh food is ideal.

Whatever food you choose for your two-week supply should be food that your family will eat and that will hold you over while grocery stores figure out appropriate supply-chain issues during the emergency period.

✦ Household Supplies

During an emergency, basic household supplies become really important as well. Cleaning supplies, especially during a disease outbreak, are necessary.

✦ Tools and Equipment

Having a few tools on hand can help your family cope in the immediate aftermath of a natural disaster. Many of these tools are good to have on hand at any time to help with regular events (like power outages) as well.

Food and Water Checklist

☐ Canned vegetables, fruits, beans, and meat

☐ Frozen vegetables, fruits, and meat

☐ Dry staples such as rice, beans, flour, pasta, and sugar

☐ Refrigerated staples such as milk, butter, cheese, and eggs

☐ Fresh produce like potatoes, apples, carrots, etc.

☐ Snacks like granola bars, cereal, candy, or chips

☐ Specialty foods, like formula, baby food, or protein drinks, for particular family members

☐ Pet food and supplies (see Disaster Pet Supply List in **PART 3** and increase to a two-week supply as appropriate)

Household Supplies Checklist

☐ Unscented liquid household chlorine bleach (5–6 percent concentration of sodium hypochlorite)

☐ Hand soap

☐ Disposable gloves

☐ Hand sanitizer

☐ Shampoo and conditioner

☐ Contact lenses solution

☐ Toothpaste

☐ Feminine supplies

☐ Dishwasher soap

☐ Laundry soap

☐ Paper towels

☐ Toilet paper

☐ Diapers and wipes

☐ Plastic sheeting and duct tape

☐ Garbage bags

The Reason for Chlorine Bleach

You can always consider additional cleaning supplies, but note that not all cleaners kill all microorganisms. This is why chlorine bleach is on the list, because it kills just about every microorganism, including Ebola. Check that your household first aid kit is up-to-date with supplies too (see Building a Proper First Aid Kit in **PART 5**).

Creating a Two-Week Survival Kit

Tools and Equipment Checklist

- ☐ Flashlights
- ☐ Extra batteries
- ☐ Fire extinguisher
- ☐ Whistle to signal for help
- ☐ Dust masks
- ☐ NOAA weather radio or battery-powered/hand crank radio
- ☐ Wrench or pliers
- ☐ Local maps
- ☐ Cell phone charger packs or solar chargers

PART 3

Preparing for Evacuation

PART 3

Preparing for Evacuation

When an emergency occurs, you might need to leave your home in a hurry, and the circumstances may not be ideal. The weather or traffic might be bad, roads or bridges might be closed, and your family might be stressed or frightened. In some instances, you may have ample time to prepare to evacuate, but in other situations, an evacuation could be immediate. Planning ahead ensures that you and your family will be able to evacuate safely and quickly when the time comes. Knowing what to bring with you and what to leave behind, how you will communicate with loved ones, where you will go and how you will get there, and how you will receive critical information from public safety officials is all key information in your preparation. Local officials will communicate the need to evacuate through various means, including traditional media, social media, and emergency alert systems.

Your Seventy-Two-Hour Survival Kit/Bug-Out Bag

Your legal documents will be important in establishing and maintaining your identity, but having an emergency supply kit may be crucial to your survival. A seventy-two-hour kit, or bug-out bag, is a great way to store important supplies in a convenient, organized way. All members of your family should have their own kit. This way, when a disaster strikes and you need to leave your home, each person can quickly grab his or her bag, be ready to leave, and have the assurance of knowing that they will have some basic items to make the relocation more tolerable.

The kits should be stored in something that is waterproof and easy to grab and carry in a hurry. Some people like to use 5-gallon buckets for their seventy-two-hour kits, while others prefer basic yet sturdy backpacks. Some disaster preparedness websites sell backpacks specially made for storing seventy-two-hour emergency supplies. The following sections list some ideas about the supplies you would want to place in your kit, but you should also customize the list for your family and its specific needs. Your kits should be stored in an easily accessible location that will be minimally affected by any damage done to your house.

Food and Water

For each person in your family, you should have a three-day supply of food and water that does not need to be refrigerated. The CDC states that bottled water is the safest choice for all uses. (See Water Supply later in this part for more information about your water supply.) If you have pets, you will need additional water for them. Here are some ideas for food items:

SNACKS:
- ☐ Protein or granola bars
- ☐ Trail mix
- ☐ Dried fruits
- ☐ Unsalted nuts
- ☐ Candy bars
- ☐ Beef jerky
- ☐ Juice boxes

NONPERISHABLE FOODS:

- ☐ Canned meats, beans, and stews
- ☐ Powdered milk
- ☐ Tuna pouches
- ☐ Dehydrated vegetables
- ☐ Dehydrated camping meals

Cooking on the Go

Dehydrated items require hot water to prepare, so you'll need access to a water supply as well as a stove or a fire.

The foods you choose to put in your seventy-two-hour kit should be easy to prepare and pack and should provide you with the calories, carbohydrates, protein, vitamins, and fats you need to survive during an emergency. Since you'll be in a high-stress environment, it will be more important than ever for you to fuel your body as best as you can and consume foods that keep your energy up. Also, remember to adjust your supply list according to your family members' needs. If you have infants, for example, be sure to include formula and diapers in one of the seventy-two-hour kits. If a family member has specific food allergies, such as nut allergies, choose that person's items accordingly.

Clothing and Bedding

In an emergency situation, having warm, dry clothing and blankets can be crucial to survival—and can also provide comfort in unfamiliar surroundings. For each member of your family, you should include the following clothing and bedding supplies, depending on your climate:

- ☐ Change of clothes, including pants, shirt, underwear, hat, hiking socks, etc.
- ☐ Fleece jacket or sweatshirt
- ☐ Comfortable hiking boots
- ☐ Raincoat or poncho
- ☐ Wool blankets or emergency heat blankets
- ☐ Tarp, to lay on damp ground or protect you from rain

You should have at least one basic set of clothes and bedding in your seventy-two-hour kit to ensure that you and your family have the right attire for any weather condition. Since clothes and bedding can take up a lot of space and add weight to your pack, consider including multipurpose items. Many survivalist websites offer clothing items that are designed to transform into emergency shelter, such as military ponchos or emergency blankets that can be used as makeshift tarp tents or sleeping bags.

Light Sources

Fuel and light are not only essential to heating food and/or seeing adequately at night; they also provide a feeling of security and normalcy in a scary situation.

✦ Flashlights

Flashlights are an excellent way to provide an immediate source of lighting in an emergency. LED flashlights are generally considered the most reliable, because incandescent bulbs can burn out suddenly or break if you drop your flashlight. In addition to not breaking easily, many LED flashlights also can last for about ten thousand hours of use. There are many different shapes and styles of flashlights, but the main difference is the size and weight of flashlight you want to carry, along with the level of brightness. If you purchase an inexpensive flashlight, the light will not be as bright as a more expensive model, and the light might be slightly off-color. Here is an overview and description of the various types of flashlights available:

- **Key ring flashlights:** These are generally more gimmicky than useful. While they are very portable and lightweight, most of them provide barely enough light to see a few feet in front of you.
- **Pocket flashlights:** Pocket flashlights are a good portable choice for an emergency. The higher-quality flashlights are able to regulate voltage, so even when the battery is losing power, the light will remain bright. They are small enough to carry in your pocket, purse, or backpack.

- **Glove compartment flashlights:** These are sometimes too large to fit easily into your pocket, and too heavy to carry in a purse or backpack. The best glove compartment flashlights offer an adjustable high and low beam; the low beam is intended for use inside the car, and the high beam is for lighting the outside of the car during emergencies.
- **Emergency crank flashlights:** These great tools are designed for emergencies. They are not dependent on the charge of a battery, they are small enough to fit into a glove compartment, and some can run for thirty to sixty minutes after one minute of cranking. They often provide other useful emergency features, like weather radios.
- **Large household flashlights:** While these are not the most portable in the event that you need to evacuate your home, they give off a great deal of light if you need to navigate your home during a power outage.
- **Rechargeable flashlights:** These are a great option while you still have power or, for those that are solar powered, while the sun is out, but they lose power quickly compared to the other options. A rechargeable flashlight is more appropriate for use in areas where a sudden power outage is dangerous or frightening, like for small children in a bathroom, because they can be located easily. Some rechargeable flashlights can recharge by being plugged into a wall outlet or via a USB cord.
- **Lithium-ion powered flashlights:** Experts recommend these for use in very cold weather and as flashlights kept at disaster shelters, because they last for a longer time under harsher circumstances.

> **Deciding On a Flashlight**
>
> When picking out your emergency flashlight, you'll want to consider what will work best for your circumstances and seventy-two-hour kit. Typically, the more powerful your flashlight is, the larger and heavier your flashlight will be. There is also a higher chance that you'll need to carry extra batteries to accommodate that power, which will add additional weight to your pack.

✦ Candles

In an emergency situation in which electricity is unavailable or limited, candles can serve as an effective, inexpensive source of light. The best kind to use are emergency candles that come in glass containers. Regular dinner candles or scented candles don't offer enough illumination. Emergency candles are specifically designed to burn for long periods; some are made to burn safely for up to 120 hours. Make sure to keep all candles on a stable, uncluttered surface, and never leave any candle unattended. Because wind can cause a candle flame to jump, don't ever place a candle near curtains or other flammable objects.

Another way to make candles safer is to use a candle lantern. Lanterns typically consist of a base, a lid, and a glass container to put the candle into. They also come with carrying handles, so the candle can be safely transported without the flame being extinguished. Some lanterns made for camping and outdoor use can also hold a standard white emergency candle. A lantern called a UCO Candlelier holds three standard emergency candles, which can be burned individually or at the same time. The tops of these lanterns also have a heat shield that can double as a small stove.

✦ Other Lighting Items

Here is a list of some other lighting supplies and accessories you might want to have in case of an emergency:

☐ Extra batteries
☐ Flares
☐ Lighter
☐ Fire extinguisher
☐ Matches in a waterproof container

Miscellaneous Supplies

There are some other items that don't necessarily fall neatly into a category but that will nevertheless be valuable additions to your seventy-two-hour kit. Here are some miscellaneous items that are helpful to include in your bug-out bag:

- ☐ Can opener
- ☐ Dishes and utensils
- ☐ Folding shovel
- ☐ Radio (with batteries)
- ☐ Pen and paper
- ☐ Ax
- ☐ Pocketknife
- ☐ Rope
- ☐ Duct tape
- ☐ Map and compass
- ☐ Unscented liquid household chlorine bleach
  (5–6 percent concentration of sodium hypochlorite)

Medication and Toiletries

Although you can't take your entire medicine cabinet along during an emergency, you should take all necessary medications with you. Although many of your supplies will be intended to last seventy-two hours, make sure you take your entire supply of any life-sustaining medications. It is wise to keep an additional three-month supply of prescription medications in your home in case of an emergency. You can also talk to your physician about writing an additional prescription for use in emergency situations.

You should put together one emergency first aid kit for your entire family, and keep it where you store your seventy-two-hour bags. When putting together your first aid kit, consider your family's medical history, such as drug allergies and risk factors, and keep these warnings in mind as you provide help. Check with your doctor for guidance on individual needs, age guidelines, and medication precautions. Here is a list of basic over-the-counter medicines and supplies you should include in an emergency first aid kit for your family:

- ☐ Antibiotic cream (like Neosporin)
- ☐ Povidone-iodine solution
- ☐ Tweezers
- ☐ Rubbing alcohol
- ☐ Cotton balls, gauze, bandages, Ace bandages, and adhesive tape
- ☐ Scissors and safety pins
- ☐ Antacids, such as Tums or Rolaids
- ☐ Thermometer
- ☐ Cotton swabs
- ☐ Sunscreen and bug spray
- ☐ 1 percent hydrocortisone cream
- ☐ Antidiarrheal medicine
- ☐ Heat pack/ice pack
- ☐ Itch medicine like calamine lotion
- ☐ Cough, cold, and allergy medicine
- ☐ Mild laxative
- ☐ Petroleum jelly
- ☐ Tooth preservation kit
- ☐ Disposable CPR face mask
- ☐ Hot-water bottle
- ☐ Eye cup and over-the-counter eyewash
- ☐ Eardrops

Save Some Space

Toilet paper rolls are big and can take up a lot of valuable space in your seventy-two-hour kit. If you remove the cardboard tube and flatten the roll, not only will you have more room in your pack, but the roll will also be easier to transport. Make sure you place the paper into a zip-top bag to protect it from the elements.

In an emergency, it's best to be prepared for any first aid need that comes your way. Not having a well-planned first aid kit will leave you vulnerable and can put you and your family in even more danger if an accident arises. Your first aid kit should always be stocked with the basics and should be easy to find near your seventy-two-hour kit.

You will also want to include a variety of toiletries to maintain your personal hygiene during a disaster and help ensure that you stay healthy and clean:

- Folding brush
- Travel-sized bottles of hand sanitizer, soap, shampoo, and dish soap
- Toothpaste
- Contact lenses case and solution
- Extra pair of glasses
- Tissues
- Toilet paper

Water Supply

When an emergency occurs, one of the most important lifesaving resources you can have is clean water. According to FEMA, a normally active person needs to drink about three quarters of a gallon of fluid per day, though individual factors apply, and if the weather is hot, this amount increases. Nursing mothers, children, and ill people may also require more water per day. The human body can survive for weeks without food, but only days without water. Whether you are displaced from your home due to a disaster situation, or an emergency causes your normal water supply to be cut off or contaminated, you will need to have an alternative source of drinking water. Water, therefore, is a crucial item to include in each family member's seventy-two-hour kit.

Running Out of Water?

If your water supplies run low, don't ration your water unless advised to do so by local authorities. Drink the amount you need today, and try to find more tomorrow. One way to minimize your body's need for water is by staying cool and decreasing your activity level.

If possible, you should store 1 gallon of water per day for each person, since water will also be needed for food preparation and personal hygiene. The FEMA website www.ready.gov advises storing at least enough water for seventy-two hours for each member of the family. If you are able, consider storing more.

Bottled water is always the safest choice. Store in the original sealed container. In an emergency if you do not have bottled water and need to prepare your own safe water, store the water in food-grade containers.

To prepare your stored water containers, follow these directions, as outlined by the CDC:

1. Thoroughly wash the containers and rinse well with water.
2. Sanitize the containers by mixing a solution of 1 teaspoon unscented liquid household chlorine bleach (that is suitable for disinfection and sanitization as indicated on the label) in 1 quart (¼ gallon) of water. With the lid on, shake the sanitizing solution in the container so that it reaches all inside surfaces of the container. Wait at least thirty seconds, and then pour out the solution. Let the sanitized container air-dry before use.

To prepare your own safe water, follow these directions:

1. Boiling water is the safest way to treat water. However, keep in mind that "boiling" does not mean just a bubble or two. You must bring the water to a rolling boil for at least one full minute. If you are worried about the water evaporating, you can put a lid on the pot to capture the steam.
2. If the water appears cloudy, filter it first through a paper towel or coffee filter. Let the boiled water cool. (For better-tasting water, pour the water back and forth between two clean containers. This increases the oxygen content of the water and improves taste. This also works for stored water.)

3. If boiling is not an option, disinfect water with unscented liquid household chlorine bleach that is suitable for disinfection and sanitization as indicated on the label.
    1. Filter the water through a paper towel or coffee filter.
    2. Follow the instructions for disinfecting drinking water that are written on the label of the bleach. For bleach with a 5–6 percent concentration of sodium hypochlorite, using a clean medicine dropper from your first aid kit, add 8 drops of unscented liquid household chlorine bleach to each 1 gallon of water.
    3. Stir the mixture well, and let it stand for at least thirty minutes. After this amount of time has elapsed, smell the water. The water should have a slight chlorine smell. If it doesn't, repeat the dosage of bleach per gallon, mix, and let it stand for another fifteen minutes.
    4. Once again, smell the water. If it still doesn't have a slight smell of bleach, discard it and find another water source.
4. Store the treated water in your sanitized containers and close tightly. Make sure not to contaminate the cap; don't touch the inside of it with your fingers.
5. Mark the outside of the container to differentiate it from the rest of your supply. Then, write the date on it so you will know when you last filled it. Keep the container in a cool, dark place.
6. Replace your water supply every six months (unless it is commercially bottled water).

Water Supply

Water Supply #1

Date of treatment: _____/_____/_____

Location of water supply: _____

Source for water supply: _____

Last time it was replenished (in days): _____

Notes: _____

_____

_____

_____

Water Supply #2

Date of treatment: _____/_____/_____

Location of water supply: _____

Source for water supply: _____

Last time it was replenished (in days): _____

Notes: _____

_____

_____

_____

Water Supply #3

Date of treatment: _____/_____/_____

Location of water supply: _____

Source for water supply: _____

Last time it was replenished (in days): _____

Notes: _____

_____

_____

_____

Water Supply #4

Date of treatment: ____/____/____

Location of water supply: _____

Source for water supply: _____

Last time it was replenished (in days): _____

Notes: _____

_____

_____

_____

Water Supply #5

Date of treatment: ____/____/____

Location of water supply: _____

Source for water supply: _____

Last time it was replenished (in days): _____

Notes: _____

_____

_____

_____

Water Supply #6

Date of treatment: ____/____/____

Location of water supply: _____

Source for water supply: _____

Last time it was replenished (in days): _____

Notes: _____

_____

_____

_____

Hidden Sources of Water

Even if you haven't stored up an emergency water supply, it is helpful to know that you can use some of the "hidden" sources of water in your home, including your hot-water heater (your drinking water system, not your home heating system) and water from ice cubes in your freezer (if water used was not contaminated). You should not drink water from toilet bowls or tanks, radiators, waterbeds, swimming pools, or spas.

When an emergency occurs, you can also turn to sources of water outside your home. Rainwater, streams, rivers, ponds, natural springs, and lakes provide potable water if you treat it. Make sure you do not use water with material floating on top or water that has an odor or dark color. Never drink floodwater. Water from the outdoors should be treated before it can be safely consumed. There are several methods of treating water, as previously outlined.

Disaster Pet Supply List

Ideally, you will not lose track of your pet in the event of a disaster; instead, your pet will stay with your family or go to a safe place for the duration of the emergency. Whether you are able to remain in your home or evacuate to a temporary location, you will need to take steps to provide for your pet's safety and comfort. The following is a list, provided by FEMA's *Ready* website, www.ready.gov, of pet emergency supplies you should prepare. As is the case with all members of your family, the top priorities should be food, water, and other essentials for survival.

- **Food:** Keep at least three days' worth of food in an airtight, waterproof container.
- **Water:** Store a supply of water (at least seventy-two hours' worth) specifically for your pets, along with the water you have prepared for yourself and your family.
- **Pet medicines:** In a waterproof container, keep an extra supply of the medicines your pet regularly takes.

- **Pet first aid kit:** Ask your veterinarian about the essential items for your pet's emergency medical needs. Most kits should contain cotton bandage rolls, bandage tape, scissors, antibiotic ointment, flea and tick prevention, latex gloves, isopropyl alcohol, and saline solution. You can also include a pet first aid book.
- **Collar with ID, harness, and leash:** Your pet's collar should include its rabies tag and identification, and it should be worn at all times. Keep a backup leash, collar, and ID tag in your pet's emergency supply kit.
- **Important documents:** Include copies of your pet's registration information, adoption papers (if applicable), vaccination documents, and medical records in the pocket of this book.
- **Crate or pet carrier:** To carry your pet securely in the event of an evacuation.
- **Sanitation items:** Include pet litter and litter box for cats, newspapers, paper towels, plastic trash bags, and household chlorine bleach to use as a disinfectant.
- **Familiar items:** If time permits, take along your pet's favorite toys, treats, or bedding in the emergency kit. Familiar items can calm your pet and decrease anxiety. If you are leaving in a hurry, bring only those items that are essential to your pet's safety.

Preparing Your Vehicle for Evacuation

It is helpful to keep your car in good condition and equipped with emergency supplies for when you have to leave your home in a hurry. Knowing that your car is ready to go in any circumstance and that you have everything you need to deal with a roadside emergency provides peace of mind during a crisis situation. At the very least, a full tank of gas, some basic knowledge, and an emergency-ready car will leave you with less to worry about. This section discusses various aspects of emergency car care and evacuation protocol.

Troubleshooting for the Car: Emergency Kit

When you have car problems at home, you most likely can turn to your garage full of tools to help you fix the problem. But oftentimes, car troubles don't occur within the convenient parameters of home—they happen on the road. Obviously, some types of car breakdown may require a professional mechanic. But sometimes, your car might have a problem that you could easily fix with the help of the proper tools.

✦ Regular Maintenance

If you are not necessarily comfortable working with wrenches, tire jacks, or coolant, that's okay. You can still be adequately prepared for an emergency situation by keeping your car in good running condition. Take your car to a trusted and qualified mechanic for regular overall checkups. According to DMV.org, some of the most important factors to check before any road trip are your GPS system, engine oil level and cleanliness, tire condition, antifreeze/coolant level, brake and power steering fluid levels, windshield washer reservoir, CV joints, electrical equipment, transmission fluid, and belts. Your car should have an oil change every 3,000–7,500 miles—check your owner's manual for specific manufacture information on this and other issues. Other parts of your car that should be checked by a mechanic routinely (as well as before an evacuation) are the following:

- ☐ Fuel and air filters
- ☐ Brakes
- ☐ Exhaust system
- ☐ Thermostat
- ☐ Heater and defroster
- ☐ Headlight, turn signals, flashing hazard, and brake lamps
- ☐ Spark plugs and cables
- ☐ Engine timing belt
- ☐ Windshield wipers
- ☐ Battery and ignition system
- ☐ Tire pressure

By having your car routinely checked by a mechanic, you can ease your mind, knowing that your car will be in good running condition if disaster strikes and you need to quickly leave your community. Regular maintenance will also ensure that you run into fewer car problems while traveling on your evacuation route.

✦ Your Emergency Tool Kit

If you or someone in your family does have some automotive know-how, it will be very useful to prepare a tool kit for dealing with potential emergencies on the road. Even if you do not have car repair knowledge, having a tool kit will not hurt and might ultimately be beneficial. Ask your mechanic what items would be most suitable for your toolbox, and store it in your car. The following are some items that may be recommended:

☐ Adjustable wrench; get a high-quality wrench that will fit practically every bolt
☐ Two screwdrivers: one flat-head, one Phillips-head
☐ Screw holders
☐ A pair of vise-grip pliers
☐ Ice scraper
☐ Gauges
☐ Tire repair kit
☐ A combination set of fuses
☐ Duct tape
☐ Jumper cables
☐ Rags for touching hot hoses and for cleanup
☐ Waterless hand cleaner
☐ Extra engine oil
☐ Premixed coolant

Safety Items

When dealing with a car emergency on the road, it is also important to take steps to ensure your own safety. Car emergencies are just as likely to happen at night as in the daytime, and weather conditions may offer poor visibility to other drivers. If, for example, you must change a tire on the road (pulling over, of course, to the safest location you can), it is crucial to make sure you are visible to oncoming traffic. The following items are useful to keep in your car. In a stressful and potentially dangerous situation, these items can protect you as well as other motorists:

- **Flares:** These are very bright and eye-catching, and signal unsuspecting drivers to slow down and be aware of a dangerous situation. *Never* light a flare if you smell a fuel leak.
- **Flashlight:** This is useful for seeing under the hood of your car, and for signaling passersby.
- **Safety triangles:** You might have seen these used to draw attention to large trucks stopped on the side of the road. Space a couple of these reflective triangles behind your car, and oncoming vehicles will be alerted to the situation.
- **Safety vest:** These are often used by nighttime runners to make drivers aware of them. If you are on the shoulder of the road fixing your car, wearing one of these could help avoid various types of accidents, such as a car hitting you, or a driver suddenly swerving into another lane upon seeing you at the last minute.
- **Flashing strobe light:** To be extra safe, a battery-powered flashing strobe will ensure that other motorists see you and are aware of your emergency situation.

Car Care Charts

This section offers a variety of checklists to help you keep track of car maintenance, troubleshoot, and decide (depending on your skill set) which maintenance projects are worth doing yourself.

Vehicle Maintenance List

Engine
☐ Engine oil filter
☐ Engine oil change

Transmission
☐ Transmission fluid change
☐ Transmission fluid filter
☐ Rear differential/transaxle lubricant change

Chassis Lubrication
☐ Fluid levels check
☐ Wheel bearings cleaning/repacking/adjustment

Tires
☐ Air pressure
☐ Tread depth
☐ Wheel balance and rotation
☐ Vehicle alignment
☐ Tire condition, including spare

Engine
☐ Performance analysis
☐ Spark plugs
☐ Air filter
☐ Fuel filter
☐ PCV valve
☐ Crankcase filter
☐ Canister filter
☐ Emission control system
☐ Exhaust analysis

Brakes
☐ Brake system inspection
☐ Brake fluid level/condition
☐ Brake system flush/bleed/adjustment
☐ Parking brake adjustment

Cooling System
☐ Level/condition
☐ Antifreeze protection
☐ Pressure test
☐ Radiator cap
☐ Hoses/clamps/thermostat
☐ Drive belts
☐ Fan and accessory belts
☐ Camshaft/timing belt
☐ Belt tension/adjustment
☐ Power flush and heater operation

Battery
☐ Electrolyte level/condition
☐ Connections/cables
☐ Battery protection treatment

Air Conditioner
☐ Performance test
☐ Discharge/evacuate/recharge
☐ A/C filter/dryer
☐ Leak test

Steering / Suspension
☐ Inspection

Car Care Charts

Vehicle Maintenance List—continued

Exhaust System
- ☐ Inspection

Lighting / Horn
- ☐ Lamp/bulbs
- ☐ Main headlamps
- ☐ Horn operation

Windshield
- ☐ Washer level/operation
- ☐ Wiper refill/blades
- ☐ Glass

State Inspection
- ☐ Safety
- ☐ Exhaust emission
- ☐ Vehicle registration

Noise, Wobble, Vibration Troubleshooter

Rear-Wheel-Drive Car
- ☐ Tires
- ☐ Differential gear (and gear oil)
- ☐ Brakes
- ☐ Drive shaft U-joint
- ☐ Wheel bearings

Front-Wheel-Drive Car
- ☐ Tires
- ☐ Brakes
- ☐ Wheel bearings
- ☐ CV joint

Four- / All-Wheel-Drive Car
- ☐ Tires
- ☐ Brakes
- ☐ Differential gear (and gear oil)
- ☐ U-joint or CV joint

Automobile Smells Troubleshooting Chart

Smell Description	Probable Cause
Burning smell from under the hood (after driving the vehicle)	Oil leak from engine onto the exhaust system
Musty, stale odor from vents (when using A/C)	Mold and bacteria growth from evaporator core in heater box under the dash
Rotten egg/sulfur smell (e.g., when stopped at a traffic light)	Catalytic converter not functioning properly
Sweet smell inside the vehicle (floor may also be damp)	Heater core failure, leaking engine coolant inside vehicle

Automobile Smoke Troubleshooting Chart

Smoke Description / Location	Probable Cause
White, thick smoke from tailpipe	Engine is burning coolant from internal leak
Bluish/white smoke from tailpipe	Engine is burning oil from piston rings or valve seals
Black smoke from tailpipe	Fuel system problem, too much fuel entering engine
After vehicle has warmed up, steam or smoke from under the hood	Coolant leak from the radiator or oil leak from engine
After vehicle warms up, steam	Heater core has leak from defroster ducts, allowing hot coolant inside vehicle

Always seek professional advice for these or any other problems with your vehicle.

Your Cars

Use this section to record some of the basic information about your car and any other vehicles your family might have. In the pocket of this book, you should also store a spare car key (if available), as well as copies of each vehicle's registration and insurance. If you have a AAA or other roadside assistance membership, also place a copy of those membership documents inside the pocket.

Car #1

Car make/model/year: _____

Car registration number: _____

Car insurance company name and telephone number: _____

Policy number: _____

AAA or other roadside assistance membership number: _____

Roadside assistance telephone number: _____

Notes: _____

_____

Car #2

Car make/model/year: _____

Car registration number: _____

Car insurance company name and telephone number: _____

Policy number: _____

AAA or other roadside assistance membership number: _____

Roadside assistance telephone number: _____

Notes: _____

_____

Car #3

Car make/model/year: _____

Car registration number: _____

Car insurance company name and telephone number: _____

Policy number: _____

AAA or other roadside assistance membership number: _____

Roadside assistance telephone number: _____

Notes: _____

_____

PART 3

What You Are Leaving Behind

Even when an urgent situation makes it necessary to evacuate your home, it often feels strange and unsettling to leave your familiar environment and possessions behind. On a practical level, too, there are factors to remember when leaving your house and the belongings within it. Even though many of these items will be too large and cumbersome to take with you, it will be helpful for you to itemize and document your possessions. They certainly are not as valuable as your life or the lives of your family members, but they have financial or sentimental value. These sections will instruct you on which documents you should keep in the pocket of this book and which document numbers or other important information you should record in the fill-in portion. Some of the possessions in your home may need to be replaced after an emergency, so taking inventory will be useful in any future insurance claims.

By knowing what you have and by carrying proof of your possessions with you, you can feel more at ease about leaving these things behind in an emergency.

Mortgage and Home Insurance

One of your most valuable assets is your home. Therefore, it is important to keep a copy of your mortgage documents, property deed or title, or renters agreement in the pocket of this book. Having easy access to these documents will make it easier to make your next mortgage or rent payment on time. During this stressful time, you're probably not thinking about your mortgage payments, but banks are not always forgiving, and your credit could be damaged if you miss a payment. You don't want this emergency situation to turn into a financial disaster as well. If you have contact information for your mortgage lender and other creditors on hand, you can call them as soon after the emergency as possible to discuss seeking a temporary deferral of payments.

If your home is fully paid for, you should also keep a copy of your mortgage discharge document in the pocket of this book. This will serve as valuable proof that you own your home outright. You might also wish to include your latest mortgage statement and tax records, or receipt of payment of these bills. If your bank offers online access to these documents, you may want to store them on a password-protected flash drive or external hard drive that you can carry with you—and you could also research storing them on a secure cloud-based service.

Your homeowners insurance policy is another document you'll want to hold on to during this time—particularly if your home sustains some degree of damage—because you will need to have proof of the coverage. (Always check ahead of time that you have adequate insurance to cover all types of emergencies.) It is also possible that your property insurance might cover temporary lodging for your family in the event of a disaster. You should store policy numbers, as well as the names and phone numbers of your lender or landlord and insurance company, in the fill-in section that follows.

Your Mortgage/Rental/Home Insurance/Utilities Information

Mortage

Mortgage lender name: _____

Mortgage lender telephone number: _____

Home loan policy number: _____

Date of last mortgage payment: ____/____/____

Is your home fully paid for? ☐ Yes ☐ No

Rent

Renter/landlord name: _____

Renter/landlord telephone number: _____

Date of last rent payment: ____/____/____

Home Insurance

Homeowners/renters insurance company: _____

Homeowners/renters insurance company telephone number: _____

Insurance policy number: _____

Date of last payment: ____/____/____

Utilities

Water/Sewerage

Water/sewerage utility company, phone number, and account information:

_____

_____

Date of last utility payment: ____/____/____

Electric

Electric utility company, phone number, and account information:

_____

_____

Date of last utility payment: _____/_____/_____

Gas

Gas utility company, phone number, and account information:

_____

_____

Date of last utility payment: _____/_____/_____

Phone/Cable/Internet

Telephone landline company, phone number, and account information:

_____

_____

Date of last payment: _____/_____/_____

Cell phone company, phone number, and account information:

_____

_____

Date of last payment: _____/_____/_____

Cable/satellite company, phone number, and account information:

_____

_____

Date of last payment: _____/_____/_____

Internet provider, phone number, and account information:

_____

_____

Date of last payment: _____/_____/_____

PART 3

Itemizing Your Possessions

While you most likely have documents proving you own/rent your home and have insurance coverage, proving ownership of your possessions is less straightforward. You may have kept the receipts for the purchase of some of the more expensive items in your home; if so, you should include those receipts in the pocket of this book.

According to FEMA's *Ready* website, www.ready.gov, another recommended step is to photograph or video the items in your house. You can do this by going from room to room, taking photos of the contents of each room. Don't forget to photograph your cars, garage, closets, drawers, and basement. You should also photograph the exterior of your house. Be sure to get photos of any antiques, heirlooms, or jewelry. Some items might require a professional appraisal to establish their worth, so talk to your insurance representative about which of your valued possessions will need to be appraised. Some insurance companies may help facilitate these appraisals for you. Keep in mind that based on the results of the appraisals, some of your possessions may need to be covered in riders to your policy.

Having proof of the items you own will be valuable in any future insurance claim you may need to make. If you take a video, you should "narrate" as you go from room to room, describing each item and any distinctive features. You can store video footage on a small computer hard drive and keep it in your seventy-two-hour kit or inside the pocket of this book.

You should also itemize your possessions in a written list. It is recommended that you write down the item's brand and model name, serial number, purchase price, and date of purchase, if known. This will take more time, but any details you have about your possessions can be helpful in a time of emergency. One useful way to categorize these belongings is to organize the list by room.

The following form is for recording any known information about your possessions. Write down what you know; don't worry if some sections are incomplete. For the purposes of this book, we will focus on furniture items, appliances, and family heirlooms. The form is organized by room, with additional customizable fill-ins for more rooms.

Kitchen

Refrigerator

Brand/model: _____   Serial number: _____

Purchase price: _____   Purchase date: ____/____/____

Dishwasher

Brand/model: _____   Serial number: _____

Purchase price: _____   Purchase date: ____/____/____

Kitchen stove

Brand/model: _____   Serial number: _____

Purchase price: _____   Purchase date: ____/____/____

Kitchen table

Brand/model: _____   Serial number: _____

Purchase price: _____   Purchase date: ____/____/____

Other valuable item name: _____

Brand/model: _____   Serial number: _____

Purchase price: _____   Purchase date: ____/____/____

Other valuable item name: _____

Brand/model: _____   Serial number: _____

Purchase price: _____   Purchase date: ____/____/____

Other valuable item name: _____

Brand/model: _____   Serial number: _____

Purchase price: _____   Purchase date: ____/____/____

Other valuable item name: _____

Brand/model: _____   Serial number: _____

Purchase price: _____   Purchase date: ____/____/____

Itemizing Your Possessions

Living Room

Couch

Brand/model: _____   Serial number: _____

Purchase price: _____   Purchase date: ____/____/____

TV

Brand/model: _____   Serial number: _____

Purchase price: _____   Purchase date: ____/____/____

Other valuable item name: _____

Brand/model: _____   Serial number: _____

Purchase price: _____   Purchase date: ____/____/____

Other valuable item name: _____

Brand/model: _____   Serial number: _____

Purchase price: _____   Purchase date: ____/____/____

Other valuable item name: _____

Brand/model: _____   Serial number: _____

Purchase price: _____   Purchase date: ____/____/____

Other valuable item name: _____

Brand/model: _____   Serial number: _____

Purchase price: _____   Purchase date: ____/____/____

Other valuable item name: _____

Brand/model: _____   Serial number: _____

Purchase price: _____   Purchase date: ____/____/____

Other valuable item name: _____

Brand/model: _____   Serial number: _____

Purchase price: _____   Purchase date: ____/____/____

Master Bedroom

Bed

Brand/model: _____   Serial number: _____

Purchase price: _____   Purchase date: ____/____/____

Other valuable item name: _____

Brand/model: _____   Serial number: _____

Purchase price: _____   Purchase date: ____/____/____

Other valuable item name: _____

Brand/model: _____   Serial number: _____

Purchase price: _____   Purchase date: ____/____/____

Other valuable item name: _____

Brand/model: _____   Serial number: _____

Purchase price: _____   Purchase date: ____/____/____

Other valuable item name: _____

Brand/model: _____   Serial number: _____

Purchase price: _____   Purchase date: ____/____/____

Other valuable item name: _____

Brand/model: _____   Serial number: _____

Purchase price: _____   Purchase date: ____/____/____

Other valuable item name: _____

Brand/model: _____   Serial number: _____

Purchase price: _____   Purchase date: ____/____/____

Other valuable item name: _____

Brand/model: _____   Serial number: _____

Purchase price: _____   Purchase date: ____/____/____

PART 3

Itemizing Your Possessions

Dining Room

Dining room table

Brand/model: _____ Serial number: _____

Purchase price: _____ Purchase date: ____/____/____

Other valuable item name: _____

Brand/model: _____ Serial number: _____

Purchase price: _____ Purchase date: ____/____/____

Other valuable item name: _____

Brand/model: _____ Serial number: _____

Purchase price: _____ Purchase date: ____/____/____

Other valuable item name: _____

Brand/model: _____ Serial number: _____

Purchase price: _____ Purchase date: ____/____/____

Other valuable item name: _____

Brand/model: _____ Serial number: _____

Purchase price: _____ Purchase date: ____/____/____

Other valuable item name: _____

Brand/model: _____ Serial number: _____

Purchase price: _____ Purchase date: ____/____/____

Other valuable item name: _____

Brand/model: _____ Serial number: _____

Purchase price: _____ Purchase date: ____/____/____

Other valuable item name: _____

Brand/model: _____ Serial number: _____

Purchase price: _____ Purchase date: ____/____/____

Additional Room #1: _____   _____

Other valuable item name: _____

Brand/model: _____   Serial number: _____

Purchase price: _____   Purchase date: ____/____/____

Other valuable item name: _____

Brand/model: _____   Serial number: _____

Purchase price: _____   Purchase date: ____/____/____

Other valuable item name: _____

Brand/model: _____   Serial number: _____

Purchase price: _____   Purchase date: ____/____/____

Other valuable item name: _____

Brand/model: _____   Serial number: _____

Purchase price: _____   Purchase date: ____/____/____

Other valuable item name: _____

Brand/model: _____   Serial number: _____

Purchase price: _____   Purchase date: ____/____/____

Other valuable item name: _____

Brand/model: _____   Serial number: _____

Purchase price: _____   Purchase date: ____/____/____

Other valuable item name: _____

Brand/model: _____   Serial number: _____

Purchase price: _____   Purchase date: ____/____/____

Other valuable item name: _____

Brand/model: _____   Serial number: _____

Purchase price: _____   Purchase date: ____/____/____

PART 3

Itemizing Your Possessions

Additional Room #2: _____

Other valuable item name: _____

Brand/model: _____ Serial number: _____

Purchase price: _____ Purchase date: ____/____/____

Other valuable item name: _____

Brand/model: _____ Serial number: _____

Purchase price: _____ Purchase date: ____/____/____

Other valuable item name: _____

Brand/model: _____ Serial number: _____

Purchase price: _____ Purchase date: ____/____/____

Other valuable item name: _____

Brand/model: _____ Serial number: _____

Purchase price: _____ Purchase date: ____/____/____

Other valuable item name: _____

Brand/model: _____ Serial number: _____

Purchase price: _____ Purchase date: ____/____/____

Other valuable item name: _____

Brand/model: _____ Serial number: _____

Purchase price: _____ Purchase date: ____/____/____

Other valuable item name: _____

Brand/model: _____ Serial number: _____

Purchase price: _____ Purchase date: ____/____/____

Other valuable item name: _____

Brand/model: _____ Serial number: _____

Purchase price: _____ Purchase date: ____/____/____

Additional Room #3: _____

Other valuable item name: _____

Brand/model: _____   Serial number: _____

Purchase price: _____   Purchase date: ____/____/____

Other valuable item name: _____

Brand/model: _____   Serial number: _____

Purchase price: _____   Purchase date: ____/____/____

Other valuable item name: _____

Brand/model: _____   Serial number: _____

Purchase price: _____   Purchase date: ____/____/____

Other valuable item name: _____

Brand/model: _____   Serial number: _____

Purchase price: _____   Purchase date: ____/____/____

Other valuable item name: _____

Brand/model: _____   Serial number: _____

Purchase price: _____   Purchase date: ____/____/____

Other valuable item name: _____

Brand/model: _____   Serial number: _____

Purchase price: _____   Purchase date: ____/____/____

Other valuable item name: _____

Brand/model: _____   Serial number: _____

Purchase price: _____   Purchase date: ____/____/____

Other valuable item name: _____

Brand/model: _____   Serial number: _____

Purchase price: _____   Purchase date: ____/____/____

PART 3

Itemizing Your Possessions

Additional Room #4: _____

Other valuable item name: _____

Brand/model: _____ Serial number: _____

Purchase price: _____ Purchase date: ____/____/____

Other valuable item name: _____

Brand/model: _____ Serial number: _____

Purchase price: _____ Purchase date: ____/____/____

Other valuable item name: _____

Brand/model: _____ Serial number: _____

Purchase price: _____ Purchase date: ____/____/____

Other valuable item name: _____

Brand/model: _____ Serial number: _____

Purchase price: _____ Purchase date: ____/____/____

Other valuable item name: _____

Brand/model: _____ Serial number: _____

Purchase price: _____ Purchase date: ____/____/____

Other valuable item name: _____

Brand/model: _____ Serial number: _____

Purchase price: _____ Purchase date: ____/____/____

Other valuable item name: _____

Brand/model: _____ Serial number: _____

Purchase price: _____ Purchase date: ____/____/____

Other valuable item name: _____

Brand/model: _____ Serial number: _____

Purchase price: _____ Purchase date: ____/____/____

PART 4

Getting Out

PART 4

PART 4

Getting Out

Evacuations can be prompted by a fire or flood at your home, or by an approaching natural disaster, such as a hurricane. Industrial accidents also may release harmful chemicals into the air, in some cases forcing residents of the surrounding area to leave their homes. Some evacuations are mandated by local officials, who have deemed the hazards to be too great for people to remain at home. In the case of such a community evacuation, local officials provide evacuation information to the public via the media, or through sirens, text alerts, emails, or telephone calls.

With some weather emergencies that have been predicted ahead of time, you may have a few days to prepare for the evacuation. However, disasters such as fires are generally not expected, and may leave you almost no time to gather your belongings and leave. If you have followed the other directions in this book, you will likely have your seventy-two-hour bug-out bag, first aid kit (see Building a Proper First Aid Kit in **PART 5**), and other crucial supplies stored in an accessible place in your house. It is also useful to prepare your family and your car for the actual transportation to a safe place.

Evacuating Your Family

In an evacuation situation, having a well-thought-out plan and being prepared are essential to getting to safety. Follow these guidelines, provided by FEMA, for emergency evacuation:

- ☐ Plan where your family will meet during an emergency evacuation. Choose more than one location, both within and outside of your immediate vicinity.
- ☐ Keep a half tank of gas in your car at all times, and a full tank if evacuation seems imminent. Gas stations may be closed during emergencies, or may be unable to operate during power outages.
- ☐ Learn about alternate routes and other means of transportation away from your area. Establish several destinations in different directions to ensure that you will have options in an emergency.
- ☐ Leave early enough to avoid being trapped by extreme weather conditions.
- ☐ Follow the evacuation routes recommended by your state government officials. Do not take shortcuts, as these streets may be blocked.
- ☐ Be on the lookout for hazards on the road, such as washed-out roads or bridges or downed power lines. Do not drive on flooded roads, or in areas where you see or anticipate flooding up ahead.
- ☐ Take your seventy-two-hour emergency kit and your first aid kit (see Building a Proper First Aid Kit in **PART 5**) if time permits you to do so safely.
- ☐ If you don't have a car, plan how you will evacuate if you need to. Make arrangements with family, friends, or local officials.
- ☐ Take your pets with you. Plan beforehand where they will stay during an emergency.

Disaster Shelters

In times of emergency, sheltering outside the hazard area can be critical, but not everyone has a safe place to stay with friends or relatives. In those instances, it's useful to use a mass shelter set up for disaster relief. Shelters provide a safe place for families affected by emergency events to reside. These shelters can offer a variety of services such as food, sleeping quarters, sanitation facilities, and medical care. Different areas have different laws regarding when and how disaster shelters can be set up and managed, but in the US, the American Red Cross is the agency most likely to partner with local government in assisting or running a disaster shelter. The American Red Cross also maintains a map and list of open and available shelters on their website at www.redcross.org/get-help/disaster-relief-and-recovery-services/find-an-open-shelter.html. You can also find open shelters near you by texting SHELTER and your zip code to 43362 or by downloading the FEMA app.

Everyone is welcome at a disaster shelter. Service animals are also welcome, but most disaster shelters do not allow family pets. However, the American Red Cross can assist you in finding a pet shelter nearby if you call your local Red Cross office. At a shelter run by the American Red Cross, you don't need a reservation—you just need to show up, and be sure to let the shelter officials know during registration if you have any special needs.

+ What to Bring to a Disaster Shelter

You should make sure to bring your seventy-two-hour survival kit, which will include your clothing and medications. It can also be good to bring some bedding if you can. You should *not* bring alcoholic beverages, illegal drugs, or weapons of any kind, as they will not be allowed on the premises and will threaten your ability to stay at the shelter should they be discovered.

✦ Services at a Disaster Shelter

Disaster shelters can offer a wide range of services to meet the communities' needs during a critical time. Along with meals and a safe place to sleep, a shelter normally provides health services for disaster-related conditions as well. They can even refill lost prescriptions and replace lost eyeglasses. Large shelters can be overwhelming due to the many organizations that may be operating in the shelter and the sheer number of people. Don't be surprised if you see National Guard service members, state and local police, disaster healthcare relief organizations, the local and state health department, and many more agencies—many of them will have their own tents or stations within a shelter. Caseworkers can help with your disaster recovery needs and can help connect you with resources in the community, even if you don't need to sleep at the shelter. Some shelters even offer childcare and laundry services.

> **Stay Healthy**
>
> It's important when staying in a disaster shelter to practice appropriate hygiene, including hand hygiene, to limit the spread of disease (see Guide to Handwashing in **PART 2** and Handwashing to Protect Yourself from Infection in the **APPENDIX**). Wash your hands after using the restroom and before eating. Cover coughs and sneezes with your elbow, not your hand. Let shelter workers know of any communicable conditions you have like MRSA or TB so they can provide appropriate services.

Your Evacuation Plan

Even if you preplanned an evacuation route for yourself and your family, it is possible that some of the roads you planned to take are closed or compromised by severe weather.

If the evacuation is mandatory and involves an emergency that affects your entire region, one of the best strategies is to listen to a local radio station on a battery-powered radio; local radio stations may provide information about evacuation routes in your area. You can also visit www.ready.gov/local for information on accessing emergency notifications specific to your region. For a mandatory evacuation, you will probably also encounter police officers directing traffic along an evacuation route, or evacuation routes will be marked by signs.

Another way to get road closure information (during a community emergency) is to call 511. This is a traveler information telephone number available in several parts of the US and Canada. During an emergency, this number provides information about roads that might not be passable. Many state government websites also have evacuation maps for coastal areas in the event of a hurricane. These maps include storm surge data and are available at all times; you might wish to print one out for your area and include it in the pocket of this book. However, you should keep in mind that this information is subject to change. When an emergency occurs, follow the evacuation orders provided at that time.

FEMA also offers text message safety tips, which can be delivered to your cell phone free of charge. You can sign up for these by texting "HURRICANE," "FLOOD," or "WILDFIRE" (or one of the other emergency topic names listed on its website) to 43362 (4FEMA). To get more information about text options, visit www.fema.gov/text-messages.

You should also sign up for any text alert systems or warning apps available from your local jurisdiction.

If you do not have access to any of these sources of information, arrange with a neighbor or family member to have them pass along evacuation route information to you.

Your Evacuation Plan

Northward Evacuation

_____

_____

_____

_____

_____

Eastward Evacuation

_____

_____

_____

_____

_____

Southward Evacuation

_____

_____

_____

_____

_____

Westward Evacuation

_____

_____

_____

_____

_____

Emergency Hotlines: National

General FEMA number: 202-646-2500

FEMA Disaster Assistance Helpline: 1-800-621-3362

Emergency Hotlines: Local

Your state's emergency management agency phone number: _____

State government website: _____

Local radio station for emergency updates: _____

Local American Red Cross phone number: _____

Your state Department of Homeland Security phone number: _____

Your local fire station phone number: _____

Your local police station phone number: _____

Your local hospital phone number: _____

Personal Contact Information

Your work phone number: _____

Your spouse's work phone number: _____

Your children's school phone numbers: _____

_____

_____

Out-of-town contact #1: _____

_____

_____

Out-of-town contact #2: _____

_____

_____

Out-of-town contact #3: _____

_____

_____

Pet Evacuation Plan

If you need to evacuate your home, it's important to make plans regarding where your pets will stay. In the case of a community emergency, some public shelters might not allow pets or might allow service animals only. Therefore, you should explore several options for sheltering your pets in the event of an evacuation. For example, you might consider family members or friends who live outside of your area who would be willing to provide lodging for your family and pets in an emergency. You can also look into pet-friendly motels or hotels outside the area, where your family and your pets can stay together. There are many websites, such as PetsWelcome.com, that can help you locate hotels or motels that accept pets. It's a good idea to establish a few possible locations ahead of time as part of your disaster plan. Other possible lodging options for pets include pet boarding facilities, such as kennels or veterinary hospitals, that are located near where your family is staying. Talk to your pet's veterinarian for information about such facilities. Remember to seek places that are close to the out-of-town locations you've established as part of your evacuation plan.

✦ Creating a "Buddy System"

An additional way to safeguard your pets in case of emergency is to establish a "buddy system" with friends, neighbors, or relatives. By planning a buddy system, you are arranging for someone you know and trust to care for or evacuate your pets if you are not able to do so. Tell your pet care buddy about your evacuation plans, and show that person where you keep your pet's seventy-two-hour supply kit. Discuss overall care and your pet's specific healthcare needs with your buddy. Establish two specific locations, one in your area and one farther away, where you can meet your pet care buddy in an emergency.

✦ At-Home Alerts

In the event of a fire or other disaster that affects your home, you will want to alert firefighters and rescue workers to the presence of pets in the house. Obtain "pets inside" stickers and put them on the doors or windows of your house. The ASPCA provides these stickers free of charge as part of its safety pack: https://secure.aspca.org/take-action/order-your-pet-safety-pack. You should fill in the best telephone contact number for yourself, too, in case an emergency separates you from your pets. If you evacuate with your pets and you have enough time, write "evacuated with pets" on the stickers so rescue workers will know.

Camping/Shelter Information

Depending on the type of emergency that has displaced you and your family from your home, you might choose to seek out a hotel, an emergency shelter, or a campsite. In some cases, if you are on the road, you might need to use your vehicle as shelter.

If you are dealing with a community emergency, your local radio stations will likely provide information about available shelters in your area. You can also request information on open shelters in your area from FEMA by texting SHELTER and your zip code to 43362. You can search for open shelters by zip code on the American Red Cross website: www.redcross.org/get-help/disaster-relief-and-recovery-services/find-an-open-shelter.html.

You may need to set up your own emergency camp outside if your home is not habitable and you don't have a place to stay. If this is the case, you will already have the seventy-two-hour kits ready for your family to use. Bring the typical necessary camping accessories such as a tent, a plastic ground cloth, and blankets. The CDC also lists the following supplies for camping. In an emergency, you should take along as many of these as you can quickly transport:

☐ Map
☐ Insect repellent
☐ Broad-spectrum sunscreen with a high sun protection factor (SPF)
☐ Compass or GPS
☐ Protective gear such as life jackets and helmets

✦ Fire Safety

It is likely that at some point during your time living outdoors, you will prepare and use a campfire, either for cooking food or providing warmth. Have an experienced member of your family build the fire. Instructions for building a campfire can be found on the US Forest Service website: https://smokeybear.com/en/prevention-how-tos/campfire-safety/how-to-build-your-campfire. You should also follow these steps for fire safety:

- When building your campfire, choose a site at least 15 feet from flammable objects; beware of overhanging tree branches.
- Make sure your campfire site has either an existing fire ring or a firepit.
- Keep a bucket of water and shovel nearby.
- Never leave a campfire unattended, and be sure to extinguish the fire completely before you leave.
- Use fireproof cooking equipment.

✦ Guard Against Carbon Monoxide Poisoning

Carbon monoxide is a colorless, odorless gas that can cause illness or death in people and animals. If you use fuel-burning equipment such as gas stoves, heaters, lanterns, or charcoal grills, the CDC cautions to *never* use them inside a tent, camper, or other enclosed shelter. This can cause a buildup of dangerous levels of carbon monoxide. A safer way to keep warm is to bring warm clothes and bedding, and, if possible, consume extra calories and fluids to prevent hypothermia.

✦ Avoid Wild Animals

Wild animals can bite you, your family members, or your pets and can transmit diseases, so it's best to avoid them as much as possible. The CDC advises that you keep any food items stored in sealed containers so as not to attract wild animals. Keep a close watch on family pets if they are with you. Check pets and family members for ticks, and remove them promptly.

Camping in a Car

If you are in your car and are unable to make it safely to an evacuation destination, you may need to stay in your car until you can get back on the road again. Because you will have your seventy-two-hour kits with you, this time will probably be much more tolerable than it would have been otherwise. Follow these directions for staying in your car listed by the CDC as part of its "sheltering in place" guidelines:

- If you are not able to get to your home or other emergency location, pull over to the side of the road, stopping your vehicle in the safest place possible. If it is sunny outside, it is better to stop under a bridge or in a shady spot to avoid becoming overheated.
- Listen to the radio regularly for updates and instructions regarding the emergency. If you have a battery-powered radio, use that, but if not, listen to your car radio regularly for updates.
- Stay where you are until you hear that it is safe to get back on the road. Follow all directions for safe routes and emergency protocol.

PART 5

First Aid Basics

PART 5

PART 5

First Aid Basics

When a disaster strikes, sometimes even the best preparation cannot prevent people from getting hurt. For this reason, it is crucial to know how to use first aid to help yourself or your family members in the event of a natural disaster, house fire, or biological or chemical event. This part is not meant to replace first aid certification classes; instead, it is meant to be an overview of the basics.

One of the best ways to provide effective first aid is to act in a calm and confident manner. If you are calm under pressure, this will help to reassure the injured person, and keep him or her as stable as possible until help arrives. The term *first aid* is named for the fact that it is the first line of medical response to an injury or illness. As such, it is often provided by nonmedical professionals, and this is okay in emergency situations. Remain calm and provide assistance to the best of your ability until help arrives. You may not be a doctor or nurse, but by performing basic first aid while waiting for help, you can help save a life.

Emergency Phone Numbers

In most emergency situations, one of the first steps you will likely take is to call your local poison control center (the American Association of Poison Control Centers help hotline number is 1-800-222-1222), your local hospital, or your family doctor. For this reason, it's very helpful to have these important telephone numbers on hand so you can access them easily (see **PART 1**). If any of your family members have serious medical problems that emergency personnel should know about, encourage them to wear a medical alert bracelet or tag with this information on it. As discussed in **PART 3** and **PART 4**, you should also formulate an evacuation plan from your home, and practice it with your kids so they will know what to do. Keep a fire extinguisher in your home, and be sure all members of your family know how to use it.

Building a Proper First Aid Kit

A good first aid kit is essential to providing the necessary medical help during an emergency. A first aid kit that is fully stocked and well organized will better equip you to be efficient and calm while assisting others. Be aware of all of the items that belong in your first aid kit, and remember to replace items that have been used up or that have reached their expiration dates.

Alert!

Make sure you keep first aid supplies out of the reach of young children and pets, as many of these supplies are potentially harmful. Store your kit in a place that is accessible to the adults in your family but can't be reached by kids or family pets, not even with the help of a chair or other climbing assistance.

+ Choosing Your Container

Your best bet for a good first aid container is something with a strong handle that can be closed securely. Be sure to mark this container "First Aid Kit." You can also buy a commercial kit from various stores, but any large, well-made plastic fishing-tackle box or toolbox works just as well and is less expensive. The ideal first aid kit should be light enough to carry in an emergency, but big enough to hold all of your necessary equipment in an organized, accessible manner. The container should be dustproof, waterproof, and sturdy enough to withstand being dropped or crushed under something.

✚ Choosing Your Location

Keep your first aid kit in a cool, dry place inside your home, preferably with your seventy-two-hour kit. Refrain from keeping it in the garage or laundry room because the extremes of moisture and temperature in those locations will be harmful to many of the items in the kit. Choose a place in your home that is central and accessible to all adults who will be using it.

Building a Proper First Aid Kit

Medicines and Ointments

Maintain this checklist to keep track of your first aid equipment and expiration dates.

☐ Oral antihistamine, such as Benadryl (diphenhydramine): _____

☐ Antibiotic ointment or cream: _____

☐ Calamine lotion: _____

☐ Antihistamine cream: _____

☐ 1 percent hydrocortisone cream: _____

☐ Povidone-iodine solution: _____

☐ Aspirin, acetaminophen, and ibuprofen: _____

☐ Antidiarrheal medication: _____

☐ Antacids, such as Tums or Rolaids: _____

☐ Mild laxative: _____

☐ Sunscreen with high SPF and bug spray: _____

☐ Sterile eyewash solution (and eye cup): _____

☐ Eardrops: _____

☐ Epinephrine auto-injector kit (if prescribed by doctor): _____

☐ Cough, cold, and allergy medication: _____

☐ Extra prescription medications (such as inhalers): _____

☐ Other: _____

☐ Other: _____

☐ Other: _____

☐ Other: _____

Be Careful of Aspirin

It is unsafe to give aspirin (even children's aspirin) to kids under the age of nineteen for any reason (unless your child's doctor prescribes it). Aspirin use in children is linked to Reye's syndrome, which is a rare but life-threatening condition that affects the liver and nervous system. The risk of developing Reye's syndrome is greatly increased when children have taken aspirin to treat flu-like symptoms or chicken pox. See also Intolerance to Medicines later in this part.

PART 5

Bandages and Dressings

- ☐ Sterile cotton balls
- ☐ Cotton-tipped swabs (such as Q-tips)
- ☐ Sterile gauze (pads and rolls)
- ☐ Elastic bandage rolls
- ☐ Extra bandage clips
- ☐ Sterile eye patches
- ☐ Ace bandages

- ☐ Antiseptic wipes
- ☐ Adhesive bandages (in various sizes)
- ☐ Adhesive tape
- ☐ Pressure bandages
- ☐ Triangular bandages
- ☐ Large foil-lined bandage (for certain kinds of burns)

Tools and Instruments

- ☐ Bulb syringe
- ☐ Medicine spoon (transparent tube marked with typical dosage amounts)
- ☐ Small paper cups
- ☐ Clean cloths and tissues
- ☐ Personal medical devices (e.g., blood glucose monitor, hearing aids)
- ☐ Medicine dropper
- ☐ Hand sanitizer
- ☐ Rubbing alcohol
- ☐ Digital thermometer (rectal thermometer for children less than three years of age)
- ☐ Small jar of petroleum jelly
- ☐ Sterile disposable gloves
- ☐ Disposable CPR face mask

- ☐ Safety pins
- ☐ Scissors (for cutting bandages)
- ☐ Tweezers
- ☐ Tooth preservation kit
- ☐ Space blanket
- ☐ Penlight
- ☐ Small pad of paper and pencil
- ☐ Emergency candle and waterproof matches
- ☐ Disposable, self-activating cold and hot packs
- ☐ Hot-water bottle
- ☐ Plastic resealable bags
- ☐ Magnifying glass
- ☐ Whistle
- ☐ Heat pack/Ice pack

PART 5

Intolerance to Medicines

When putting together your first aid kit, consider your family's medical history, such as drug allergies and risk factors, and keep these warnings in mind as you provide help. Check with your doctor for guidance on individual needs, age guidelines, and medication precautions. For instance, aspirin, ibuprofen, and other nonsteroidal anti-inflammatory drugs (NSAIDs) may cause stomach bleeding and kidney damage even when taken in the proper dosage. For those taking NSAIDs for an extended period, the risk of bleeding is usually higher in people over the age of sixty-five, those with stomach ulcers, and people taking certain medications (such as blood-thinning medications or steroids). Acetaminophen poses a risk of severe liver damage when taken in doses higher than recommended, or when taken by a person who consumes three or more alcoholic drinks per day. Acetaminophen is an ingredient in many over-the-counter (OTC) medicines, so be sure to check the labels of all medicines to make sure you are not exceeding the general recommended safe daily dose of 3 grams, or 3,000 milligrams, for a healthy adult.

Universal Precautions

When performing first aid, there is a risk of disease transmission through bodily fluids. As an emergency first aid provider, you should try to follow some standard precautions and use personal protection equipment like gloves, a CPR barrier, and eye protection. Universal precautions shield first aid providers from exposure to HIV, hepatitis B and hepatitis C, and other blood-borne germs that are transmitted through blood, certain bodily fluids, and the tissues of an infected person. You should also take universal precautions when dealing with cerebrospinal (from the lining of the brain and spinal cord), synovial (joint), peritoneal (abdominal), pericardial (heart), and amniotic (pregnant uterus) fluids. These precautions do not apply to body fluids like saliva, urine, sweat, tears, nasal fluid, or feces, unless they contain blood.

Professional universal precautions include the following:

1. Wash your hands before and after providing any medical help.
2. Wear gloves whenever you are exposed to another person's blood, body secretions, or tissues, even if the person is a family member.
3. Wear a face mask and body gown whenever there is a possibility of blood dripping onto you.
4. Throw away all contaminated sharp tools in an appropriate, puncture-proof container.
5. Dispose of all contaminated equipment in a designated biohazard container.

As a layperson responding in an emergency situation, you may not have all of the exact equipment needed for universal precautions. However, these professional guidelines can help point you in the right direction and enable you to protect yourself from infectious disease. You should try to follow these guidelines as closely as you can. Remember, you should use a protective barrier when giving first aid to anyone, even if you know that person well. It is simply common sense and good first aid practice to avoid contact with an unknown potential source of infection. By using barriers and following universal precautions to the best of your ability, you can provide effective care for the injured person while protecting yourself against disease.

Emergency Response

Most people know at least some information about cardiopulmonary resuscitation (CPR) and understand its importance in saving lives. When a bystander witnesses a person collapsing or going into cardiac arrest (called "witnessed arrest"), CPR needs to begin immediately to be most effective. Immediate CPR can double or triple the chances of survival after cardiac arrest. This is why it is important for you and members of your family to become certified in CPR and automated external defibrillators (AEDs) and to renew certification as needed. By learning this valuable skill, you can help save lives, minimize disability, restore health, and even reverse clinical death in an emergency.

The Basics of First Aid

Emergency first aid consists of crucial steps, which involve checking basic body functions. Basic life support, or CPR, along with early defibrillation, has been shown to improve long-term survival after a cardiac arrest. Although this book describes the basic steps for performing first aid and CPR, it should not be considered a substitute for instruction. Instead, it should be used as an introduction to CPR and first aid, to be followed by formal training. You can find CPR and first aid classes in your area by calling the American Heart Association (AHA) or the American Red Cross.

You can easily remember the steps of first aid by thinking of the letters *DR ABC*—this stands for danger, response, airway, breathing, and CPR.

- **Danger:** Make sure it is safe to approach the person who has fallen. Use protective equipment and follow standard precautions. Steer clear of obvious hazards.
- **Response:** Check if the person is responsive by tapping her on the shoulder and shouting, "Are you okay?" For a baby, shout and flick the bottom of his foot to gain a response. Never shake a baby or child. If it's evident the person needs help, call 911 or ask someone to call 911.
- **Airway:** Open the airway. The following steps explain how to open the airway:

Place one hand on the forehead and tilt the head backward. Place your other hand underneath the bony part of the chin and lift the chin upward. This maneuver is known as a "head tilt chin lift" and will move the tongue away from the back of the airway, enabling the victim to breathe. If you suspect the victim may have a neck or back injury, then the jaw-thrust maneuver should be used instead. With this technique, the head is not tilted backward, so there is less movement of the victim's neck. Take a look at Neck and Back Injuries in **PART 6** for information on how to perform the jaw-thrust technique and how to manage an unconscious victim with a possible neck or back injury.

For babies, the procedure to open the airway is not the same as for adults and older children. The neck and throat of a baby are still developing, and the structures move differently than those of adults. The correct way to open a baby's airway is to place the head in a neutral position. Give the baby's head a slight tilt backward with two fingers. In addition, take care not to apply any pressure to the baby's neck; this can also block the airway.

- **Breathing:** Check for regular, normal breathing for a maximum of ten seconds.
- **CPR:** The most important decision you need to make is whether to commence CPR. If the unconscious victim *is not* breathing, then immediately commence CPR. It is vital that EMS be kept informed of the victim's condition. Emergency services must be notified if the victim is not breathing so they can arrange an appropriate emergency medical response.

If the victim *is* breathing normally, perform a quick check to see if there is any major life-threatening bleeding (see Severe Bleeding in **PART 6**). If you don't suspect a neck or a back injury, the victim should be placed in the recovery position (see Recovery Position later in this part) to further protect the airway.

✚ What Is CPR?

Cardiac arrest is not caused by a single problem, but can be triggered by various underlying issues. In this book, only lay-rescuer techniques and methods will be described. If you don't want to do rescue breathing because you don't have a barrier, properly completed chest compressions will be enough. When you see an adult or teen suddenly collapse, you should take the following steps.

How to Perform CPR

Let's take a look at how to perform CPR on a victim of sudden cardiac arrest. We have already assessed danger, response, airway, and breathing, and established that the victim is not breathing normally. You must ensure that EMS has been called and then begin performing chest compressions.

For untrained bystanders treating adult and teen victims who suddenly collapse, the AHA now recommends performing chest compressions only and not stopping to attempt rescue breaths. High-quality chest compressions are the most important part of CPR, and it is vital that they are started quickly.

✚ How to Give Effective Chest Compressions

To deliver high-quality chest compressions:

1. Kneel at the victim's side, parallel to his chest.
2. Place the heel of one hand in the middle of the victim's chest between the nipples.
3. Place your other hand on top of the first hand so your hands are parallel.
4. Push down to a depth of at least 2 inches (approximately 5 centimeters). Allow the chest to rebound to the normal level, although it might be lower.
5. Fully release and let the chest come back up.
6. Repeat and aim for 100–120 chest compressions per minute (maximum of two chest compressions per second). (The Bee Gees' song "Stayin' Alive" will help with timing.)

Keep your elbows locked and use your upper body weight to deliver effective chest compressions. Ensure that you let the chest wall recoil fully after each compression and do not lean on the victim's chest. See CPR for Children later in this part for CPR information specific to children.

The delivery of effective chest compressions requires a significant amount of energy from the rescuer. Evidence shows that chest compression quality decreases after only one to two minutes of CPR. If more than one rescuer is available, trade performing CPR approximately every two minutes.

Don't Worry about Rib Fractures

It is common for effective chest compressions to cause fractures of the victim's ribs and sometimes even his breastbone (sternum). Around a third of victims who receive CPR will sustain at least one rib fracture. If you feel rib fractures when performing CPR, recheck your hand position and the depth of chest compressions, but do not stop CPR!

Continue performing CPR until EMS arrives. It can be off-putting if you hear or feel a rib fracture during CPR, but remember, you could save the victim's life. Any rib fractures you cause can be treated at a later date, but only if the victim is alive!

✦ How to Give Effective Rescue Breaths

If you are a trained rescuer and willing to deliver rescue breaths, then perform two rescue breaths after each set of thirty compressions. Continue this cycle of thirty chest compressions to two rescue breaths.

1. Open the victim's airway by tilting the head backward and lifting the chin.
2. Pinch the nose to prevent air leaking out.
3. Take a regular breath and make a seal over the victim's mouth, using a disposable resuscitation face shield if available.
4. Blow into the victim's mouth for approximately one second; do not overinflate the victim's lungs, as this could cause air to go into the stomach and the victim to vomit.
5. Deliver two rescue breath attempts in total, then immediately resume chest compressions.

If two trained rescuers are present, one can perform chest compressions, followed by the other delivering rescue breaths, still at a ratio of thirty chest compressions to two rescue breaths. This two-person technique minimizes any interruptions in chest compressions.

Continue providing CPR (either chest compressions only, or—if trained—chest compressions with rescue breaths) until the arrival of a defibrillator or emergency medical help. If a defibrillator is available, attach it to the victim and follow the instructions (see What Is an AED? later in this part). When EMS arrives, they may ask you to assist by continuing chest compressions while they perform advanced medical interventions.

The victim may vomit when you are performing CPR. If this happens, don't panic. It does not mean that you've done anything incorrectly. An unconscious victim can lose control of his stomach contents and may vomit. If the victim vomits when you are performing CPR, turn him onto his side to allow the vomit to drain away from the airway. Then turn him back and resume CPR as quickly as possible.

✚ When to Stop CPR

CPR needs to be performed continuously for it to be effective. Stop CPR only if:

- The victim shows signs of life and is breathing normally.
- EMS arrives and asks you to stop.
- The environment becomes too unsafe for you to remain on scene, and you cannot safely move the victim.
- You become physically exhausted and unable to continue. Remember you are the most important person in any emergency situation. If you become exhausted and bystanders are present, show them how to perform chest compressions so they can take over.

CPR for Children

Performing CPR on children has its own set of rules, since their physical systems and bodies are more delicate than those of adults.

✚ Child CPR (Ages 1 to Puberty)

When performing CPR on a child, chest compressions require less force than on an adult. It is acceptable to use one hand when delivering compressions on a very small child. However, a large child may require the two-handed technique to achieve effective chest compression depth. Place the child on his or her back. Deliver chest compressions at the same rate as for an adult victim (100–120 chest compressions per minute) and in the same location (center of the chest). The depth of chest compressions on a child should be approximately one third the depth of the chest—2 inches for children, 1.5 inches for babies.

Rescue breaths for a child will require less force than for an adult victim. Ensure the child's airway is open and make a seal over her mouth. Use a disposable resuscitation face shield if available. Blow air in until the child's chest rises, then stop. Deliver two rescue breath attempts before immediately resuming chest compressions. If two rescuers are present, one can perform chest compressions and the other can perform rescue breathing in order to minimize the interruption in chest compressions.

✚ Baby CPR (Ages 0–1)

When performing CPR on a baby, chest compressions should be done by placing the pads of two fingers in the center of the baby's chest. Deliver chest compressions at the same rate as for an adult victim (100–120 chest compressions per minute). The depth of chest compressions on a baby should be approximately one third the depth of the chest—1.5 inches.

When performing rescue breaths on a baby, you may need to make a seal over the baby's mouth and nose. Take care not to extend the neck when performing rescue breathing, as this will close off the airway. Blow in only until the baby's chest rises; this will require just a small puff of air. Do not overinflate a baby's lungs.

Problems with CPR

The AHA has determined some of the more common problems with lay-rescuer CPR. Some of these are as follows:

- Compressions that are interrupted too frequently
- Compressions that are too slow or too shallow

✚ Other Concerns

Another possible obstacle to lifesaving CPR is hesitancy on the part of bystanders to perform it because it seems too difficult or complicated. For this reason, the AHA has tried to simplify the steps by making the compression-ventilation ratio the same for people of all ages: 30/2. The same update has been made for chest compressions in children and adults.

Fear of contracting an infectious disease through mouth-to-mouth resuscitation might be another reason bystanders are reluctant to perform CPR. However, recent data has suggested that the transmission rate of infection is very low. The use of a barrier device, such as a CPR mask, is still advised as part of standard precautions. If you still feel uncomfortable giving mouth-to-mouth ventilations, you can at least call for help and begin chest compressions immediately. Remember that any CPR efforts you make can possibly save a life.

What Is an AED?

An automated external defibrillator (AED) is a small, portable electronic device that administers an electric shock to disrupt an abnormal heart rhythm and "reset" the heart to resume a normal, effective rhythm. An AED shock cannot restart a stopped heart; the heart must have a rhythm, even if it is irregular. The AED will automatically diagnose any cardiac arrhythmia when it is attached by leads to an unconscious person. If the AED detects a lethal heart rhythm and recommends that you deliver a shock, you can then treat the person with the AED shock, or defibrillation. This may interrupt the abnormal electrical activity and allow the heart to reestablish a normal and effective rhythm. Many first aid, first-responder, and CPR classes provide instruction on how to use an AED.

Recovery Position

The recovery position is a technique used in first aid to protect the airway in people who are breathing but unconscious. This includes people in any of the following situations:

- Anyone over the age of one year who has resumed breathing after being given CPR (also see the sidebar, Special Cases, later in this part)
- Those who are very intoxicated and at risk of ceasing to breathe
- People who are near-drowning
- Cases where a person may have been poisoned

An unconscious person who is lying faceup is in a position that may result in blockage of the airway. In the faceup position, the tongue may relax to the back of the throat, and fluids such as blood and vomit can collect in the back of the throat and obstruct the airway. In addition, the esophagus of a person lying faceup tilts down slightly from the stomach toward the throat. When combined with the loss of muscle control that happens when someone is unconscious, this tilting of the esophagus can lead to something known as passive regurgitation. In passive regurgitation, the contents of the stomach come up into the throat. Aside from causing airway blockage, fluid collecting in the back of the throat can flow down into the lungs. Stomach acids in regurgitated fluids can cause damage to the lungs; this is known as aspiration pneumonia. In many cases, the actual injury that rendered a person unconscious will not be fatal, but passive regurgitation or aspiration pneumonia will be.

One very common cause of death is excessive alcohol intake that leads to unconsciousness and some or all of the events just described. This is why it is important to place an unconscious, breathing person in the recovery position. When a person is placed in the recovery position, the force of gravity keeps the tongue from blocking the airway and prevents fluids from flowing in the wrong direction. This, along with raising the chest above the ground, protects the person while helping him to breathe.

✛ Steps for Proper Positioning

In keeping with the DR ABC steps mentioned earlier, your first steps should be to evaluate the area for safety before you approach the unconscious person and then check for response. Next, evaluate the person for airway, breathing, and CPR in the ways described. If the person does not need CPR, or if you've already used CPR to initiate breathing, then put the person in the recovery position. Do not use this position if you see signs of spinal or neck injury; refer to Neck and Back Injuries in **PART 6** for a modified position for these injuries. See the following Special Cases sidebar if you are assisting a pregnant woman, a person with wounds to the torso, or a baby. If you see no signs of spinal or neck injury, you should put the person in what is called the lateral recovery position:

1. With the person lying on her back with legs straight out, kneel on one side, facing her. Place the person's arm that is closest to you perpendicular to her body, with her palm facing up. Then place the other arm across the person's body, resting the back of her hand on her cheek closest to you. Hold it there.
2. With your other hand, bend the leg that is farthest from you upward to a right angle, with the foot flat on the floor; the knee should be elevated.
3. Keeping the back of the victim's hand against her cheek, reach behind the far knee to carefully roll the victim toward you on her side.
4. Continue to monitor breathing and vital signs.

People who stay in this position for long periods of time may sustain nerve compression, so you should move the person from one side to the other side every thirty minutes if emergency rescue is taking a long time to arrive.

✚ Position for Spine or Neck Injury

As mentioned, if the person has suffered a spinal injury, any further movement of the injured neck carries a risk of causing permanent paralysis or other injuries, so any movement should be limited.

The only reason to place a person with possible spinal injury in the recovery position is if you need to drain vomit from the airway. See Neck and Back Injuries in **PART 6** for a full discussion of these injuries, including when to use a modified recovery position.

Special Cases

A pregnant woman who is unconscious should always be placed in the recovery position on her left side. A person with wounds to the torso should be placed with the wounds closest to the ground to reduce the risk of blood collecting in the lungs. Unconscious babies who are less than a year old should be placed in a modified recovery position: Hold the infant facedown along your forearm, his head tilted slightly downward, to stop the tongue from blocking the airway or the infant inhaling vomit. Support the head and neck with your other hand. In all cases, you should continue to check the person's level of response, pulse, and breathing until professional help arrives.

Choking

Choking happens when something becomes stuck in the throat and partly or completely obstructs the airway. Some signs of choking include the following:

- Pointing to the throat, hands crossed on throat (this is a universal sign of choking)

- Coughing or gasping
- Signs of panic
- Inability to speak
- Flushed face that is turning pale or bluish
- Passing out

When you think someone might be choking, you should ask, "Are you choking?" If the person is able to verbally answer you, he might—with your encouragement—be able to cough out the food on his own. Continue to monitor, and call EMS if the symptoms do not quickly resolve. A person who is actually choking won't be able to talk and will need your help. If the person is not able to answer you, is unable to make noise or breathe well, or is unconscious, you should first call 911, and then, if the person is conscious, begin the Heimlich maneuver as described in the following section. If the person is not conscious, lay him on his back. Check the person's mouth for any signs of a visible blockage, and try to extract it with a sweep of your finger. If you are not able to remove the obstruction, begin CPR. Continue to check inside the person's mouth for any signs of the blockage, as the chest compressions of CPR may force it out.

Heimlich Maneuver

The Heimlich maneuver is a technique by which you deliver abdominal thrusts to yourself or another person who is choking. The Heimlich maneuver is advised for use in clearing a blocked airway in conscious adults and children over the age of one. It is not intended to be used on infants under a year old. The act of the abdominal thrust lifts the diaphragm and expels air from the lungs, similar to a coughing action. This forces the foreign body up and out of the body through the mouth.

These are the steps for performing the Heimlich maneuver on a choking, conscious person:

1. Stand behind the person, wrap your arms around the waist, and tip the person slightly forward.

2. Make a fist with one hand and place that hand slightly above the person's belly button.
3. Grasp your fist with your other hand and press forcefully into the abdomen with quick, upward thrusts, using enough force as though you were trying to lift the person up.
4. Continue the thrusts until the obstruction is expelled or EMS arrives.

To clear an airway blockage of a person who is obese or pregnant, place your fists closer to the chest, right above the joining of the ribs at the base of the breastbone. Then follow the Heimlich maneuver steps.

✛ Self-Administered Heimlich Maneuver

If you are choking and no one else around you is able to perform the Heimlich maneuver, you may have to administer it to yourself. The steps to performing the Heimlich maneuver on yourself are as follows:

1. Place your fist just slightly above your navel.
2. Grasp your fist with your other hand, bend over a hard surface like a chair or countertop, and thrust your fist inward and upward.

Minor Wounds (Cuts and Grazes)

Cuts and grazes are common minor injuries in both adults and children. Our skin provides a protective barrier to prevent infection from entering our bodies. A minor wound causes a break in the skin, leading to the risk of infection entering the wound and potentially spreading into the bloodstream. First aid for minor wounds should focus on keeping the wound clean and preventing it from becoming contaminated with dirt or other sources of infection.

Many minor wounds can be cared for at home, using first aid measures without seeking medical attention. However, medical attention should be sought for deep or complicated wounds (see sidebar, When to

Seek Medical Advice). Minor wounds will begin to heal within a day or so following the injury. If a wound doesn't start healing, you should seek medical advice, as this could indicate a foreign body in the wound or the presence of infection.

When to Seek Medical Advice

You should seek urgent medical advice for a wound if you are concerned, or if the wound has any of the following features:

- There is dirt or a foreign object in the wound (for example, a shard of glass), or the wound was caused by something very dirty or rusty
- The wound is particularly deep or is bleeding heavily
- The wound edges do not come together
- The wound has rough, jagged edges
- The wound is to the face, as there is a risk of scarring
- There is any evidence of infection
- The wound was caused by a bite from an animal or human
- The wound is a puncture wound
- The victim's tetanus immunizations are not up-to-date
- The wounded area feels numb

✚ Signs and Symptoms of an Infected Wound

- Pain or tenderness
- A spreading red area around the wound
- Swelling or warmth in the affected area
- Pus discharging from the wound
- High temperature (fever)
- Swollen lymph nodes

Do not delay seeking medical attention if you are concerned a wound is infected. If left untreated, the infection could spread to the bloodstream and cause blood poisoning (septicemia).

✚ First Aid Treatment for a Minor Wound

1. If the wound is bleeding, ask the victim to apply direct pressure to stem the bleeding.
2. Elevate the wound if it is on an arm or leg.
3. Wash your hands with soap and water, and put on disposable gloves.
4. Thoroughly wash the wound under running tap water.
5. If running water is not available and you have a first aid kit, use antiseptic wipes to clean the wound.
6. If available, and as long as the victim does not have any allergies to antibiotics, apply a topical antibiotic ointment or cream.
7. Cover the wound with a sterile dressing to protect it from infection; small wounds may be covered with an adhesive dressing, while larger wounds may require a bandage.
8. Seek medical advice if concerned (see previous sidebar, When to Seek Medical Advice).

Always Think about Tetanus

Tetanus is a severe infection caused by bacteria that lives in soil and animal waste. The tetanus germ can enter the body through cuts and scrapes contaminated with dirt. Children are now routinely vaccinated against tetanus. Immunization requires multiple shots to be given, and adults require a booster shot every ten years as part of their vaccine schedule. Any victim with a dirty wound should be advised to seek medical attention for proper wound cleaning and an assessment of her or his tetanus risk.

PART 5

Soft-Tissue Injuries (Sprains and Strains)

A soft-tissue injury occurs when there is damage to muscle, tendons, or ligaments. These structures are known as the soft tissues. Common soft-tissue injuries include sprains and strains (see sidebar, Medical Terminology, for the difference between a sprain and a strain).

Soft-tissue injuries can occur due to abnormal twisting movements or the overstretching of muscles. These types of injuries are common among athletes; however, anyone can sustain a soft-tissue injury, for example, following a simple trip or fall at home. Soft-tissue injuries can be painful and cause a significant amount of swelling. Distinguishing between a soft-tissue injury and a broken bone is challenging, even for a medical professional. In first aid, you should not attempt to diagnose the type of injury the victim has sustained. All soft-tissue injuries should be evaluated by a medical professional who can provide a thorough assessment including an X-ray of the injury.

> **Medical Terminology**
>
> A *sprain* occurs when there is damage to a ligament. Ligaments are tough bands of soft tissue that connect bones together. A *strain*, on the other hand, occurs when a muscle is overstretched, leading to damage to the muscle fibers or tendon. A tendon connects muscle to bone.

Signs and symptoms of a soft-tissue injury include:

- Pain on movement of the area
- Tenderness
- Bruising and swelling (may not develop immediately)
- Muscle cramps or spasm
- Reduced joint mobility

✚ First Aid Treatment for a Soft-Tissue Injury

You can remember the correct first aid treatment for a soft-tissue injury by using the acronym PRICE:

1. **P**rotect the area from further injury.
2. **R**est the injury.
3. **I**ce the injury to reduce swelling and pain.
4. **C**ompress the injury gently with a bandage or joint support.
5. **E**levate the limb to reduce swelling and pain.

Ice should not be applied directly to the skin, as doing this can cause freeze burns. Many varieties of commercial ice packs are available. Only apply ice for a maximum of fifteen to twenty minutes every two to three hours.

Severe soft-tissue injuries can cause significant damage to a joint and take several weeks to start healing. It is important to seek advice from a qualified medical professional regarding evaluation, rehabilitation, and physical therapy, especially if the victim is planning to return to an athletic activity. In rare cases, surgery may be required for severe or recurrent sprains.

Splinters

A splinter occurs when a small fragment of a larger object becomes embedded in the skin. As anyone who works outside knows, wood splinters are common, although glass, metal, and plastic can also cause splinters. All splinters should be removed as soon as possible after they occur, as they can migrate farther into the body tissues and cause swelling or infection. Small splinters are often easily removed at home using tweezers; however, deep splinters, splinters lodged under a fingernail or toenail, or splinters that have been embedded for a period of time will require medical assistance to remove properly.

Signs and symptoms of a splinter include:

- Visible embedded object
- Puncture wound
- Pain
- Swelling around the area

For signs and symptoms of an infection, see Signs and Symptoms of an Infected Wound earlier in this part.

✚ First Aid Treatment for a Splinter

Only attempt to remove superficial splinters. Seek urgent medical attention for deep or complicated splinters.

1. Clean the area with running water and soap.
2. Put on disposable gloves.
3. Using clean tweezers (ideally a sterile disposable set), attempt to remove the splinter back along the same angle at which it entered the skin.
4. After removing the splinter, clean the area again and cover with a sterile dressing.

Splinters and Tetanus

There is a risk of tetanus from splinters. Seek medical advice if the victim has sustained a splinter and her tetanus immunizations are not up-to-date or she is unsure about her tetanus immunization history.

Seek medical help if you are unable to remove the splinter, you have concerns that there is still an object embedded in the wound, or the area shows signs of infection.

Blisters

A blister occurs when a pocket of fluid forms in the superficial layer of the skin. This fluid causes a bulge underneath the skin. Excessive friction on the skin commonly causes blisters (for example, by wearing ill-fitting shoes). The hands and feet are most prone to developing blisters, but they can occur on any part of the body. The fluid produced by a blister is designed to cushion and protect the underlying skin from further damage and to aid healing. Bursting a blister will remove this protective layer and also increase the risk of infection developing (see sidebar, Don't Burst Blisters).

> **Don't Burst Blisters**
>
> Blisters, like open wounds, cause a break in the protective layer of the skin and are at risk of becoming infected. For this reason, it is advised not to burst blisters, as this will create a route of entry for harmful germs. If a blister shows signs of becoming infected, seek medical help.

✚ First Aid Treatment for a Blister

1. Clean and dry the affected area.
2. Cover the blister with a sterile dressing or specialized blister bandage (see Bandaging a Blister in the **APPENDIX**). Don't apply the adhesive directly over the blister, as this will cause damage when the dressing or bandage is removed.
3. Seek medical advice if the blister shows signs and symptoms of infection.
4. It is generally advised not to burst blisters (see sidebar, Don't Burst Blisters). If a blister bursts by itself, ensure the area is cleaned and covered with a sterile dressing to prevent infection.

It is always better to prevent a blister from occurring in the first place. Simple steps such as wearing the correct footwear can reduce the chances of developing a blister. If you feel an area of friction when walking (for example, on the heel of the foot), you can apply a bandage over the area to protect the skin and prevent a blister from developing.

Foreign Body in the Eye

Our eyes are delicate and vulnerable to contamination from foreign bodies such as grit, dust, metal, and other small objects. Wearing appropriate eye protection is essential when carrying out tasks that may cause eye injuries. A foreign body in the eye can cause permanent damage to the victim's vision and increase the risk of infection developing in the eye. Superficial foreign bodies that have not penetrated into the eyeball can often be washed out with running water or eyewash. If the surface of the eye is damaged or has been penetrated by the object, then specialist medical help will always be required to prevent loss of sight. A foreign body in the eye can scratch the surface of the eye (known as the cornea) and cause symptoms for several days after the object has been removed. Our eyes are precious, and damage to vision can have serious long-term consequences for a victim. It is always best to seek advice and undergo a professional eye examination to ensure the foreign body has not damaged the eye.

Signs and symptoms of a foreign body in the eye may include:

- A gritty sensation when blinking
- Pain, worse when moving the eye
- Eye watering
- Bloodshot eye
- Visual disturbance or loss of vision

✚ First Aid Treatment for a Foreign Body in the Eye

1. Wash your hands, and put on disposable gloves.
2. Inspect the eye to find the foreign object. Only attempt to remove superficial small objects with irrigation.
3. Attempt to flush out the object by pouring a gentle stream of clean water or sterile eyewash solution into the inner corner of the eye.
4. Do not rub the affected eye or attempt to remove the object with tweezers or a cotton swab.
5. If the object is large or sharp or you are unable to remove it quickly, seek medical advice.

6. Seek urgent medical attention if the object appears to have penetrated the eyeball or there are problems with vision. (For more detail see Irrigating an Eye to Remove a Foreign Body in the **APPENDIX**.)

Knocked-Out Teeth

In a violent disaster, a blow to the face or mouth can result in an adult tooth becoming dislodged and falling out. A knocked-out adult tooth is a dental emergency and requires prompt treatment from a dental professional in order to save the tooth. Be aware that other injuries may exist in a victim with a knocked-out tooth. A direct blow to the face or the jaw can cause a fracture to the bones in the face. When dealing with a knocked-out tooth, your main aim is to try to save the tooth to enable its reimplantation by a dentist.

The best place for a knocked-out tooth is back in the socket; however, if this is not possible, then milk can be used to preserve the damaged tooth. In some cases, a knocked-out tooth might be accidently swallowed or even go into the victim's airway. If this occurs, the victim will need urgent medical assistance in order to find and remove the tooth.

✚ First Aid Treatment for a Knocked-Out Tooth
1. Hold the tooth by the upper half (crown). Do not touch the bottom half (root) of the tooth.
2. If the tooth is visibly dirty, briefly and gently wash with running water; however, do not scrub the tooth or use soap.
3. If possible, place the knocked-out tooth back into the socket. Do not force the tooth in if you feel resistance or the victim experiences significant pain.
4. If unable to replace the tooth, place it in a tooth preservation solution (from your first aid kit) or cold milk to preserve it until dental help can be sought.
5. Do not use regular tap water, as this is harmful to the tooth.
6. Seek emergency dental help as soon as possible to give the victim the best chance of having the tooth reimplanted.

Nosebleeds

Nosebleeds are common in both adults and children, and a highly stressful situation may aggravate them. Our noses have a rich blood supply that helps warm the air we breathe in. Nosebleeds can occur spontaneously or following irritation or trauma to the nose. People who take blood-thinning medications are more at risk of developing nosebleeds, and these nosebleeds can be difficult to stop. If a nosebleed does not stop after twenty minutes, seek medical attention; the blood vessel causing the nosebleed may need to be treated to stop further bleeding. In addition, although rare, recurrent nosebleeds can be a sign of a more serious underlying medical problem and should be investigated by a medical professional.

Rarely, a serious nosebleed can be life-threatening and can lead to shock from excessive blood loss. Always be aware of the potential for shock, and call EMS if the bleeding is uncontrollable or the victim goes into shock. Patients who take medication to thin their blood are more at risk of having a serious nosebleed and requiring medical intervention to stop the bleeding.

Lean Forward Not Backward

Victims with a nosebleed should lean forward, not backward. By leaning forward, the victim will enable the blood to drain out the nose and not down into the throat. Leaning backward can cause the victim to swallow blood, and this can cause vomiting.

✚ First Aid Treatment for a Nosebleed
1. Lean the victim forward.
2. Ask the victim to pinch the soft part of his nose (and breathe through his mouth) for a minimum of ten minutes without releasing.
3. If the bleeding is ongoing after the first ten minutes, ask the victim to reapply pressure for ten more minutes.
4. A cold compress or ice pack can be applied to the nose to reduce blood flow to the area.

5. If the nosebleed has not stopped after twenty minutes, seek urgent medical advice.

Once the nosebleed has stopped, the victim should not pick or blow his nose for several hours. If a victim has recurrent nosebleeds, then he should seek medical attention to investigate the underlying cause of the bleeding.

✚ Blood-Thinning Medication

Some people take blood-thinning (anticoagulant) medication for heart conditions or following a blood clot. Examples of these medications include warfarin (Coumadin), rivaroxaban (Xarelto), apixaban (Eliquis), and dabigatran (Pradaxa). These medications can make nosebleeds very difficult to stop, and the patient may require medical intervention to find and stop the bleeding blood vessel. Contact your doctor to discuss managing your nosebleed risks on anticoagulants.

Fainting

Many of us have witnessed, or experienced, fainting episodes, and they may quite possibly occur during a disaster or evacuation. So, what exactly causes a faint? A faint occurs when the blood supply to the brain is temporarily interrupted. As a result, the brain does not receive enough oxygen or nutrients. This leads to a temporary loss of consciousness known as a faint, and the victim often falls to the floor.

Medical Terminology

The medical term for fainting is *syncope*.

A fainting victim usually recovers quickly once lying down, since being horizontal on the floor improves the blood supply to the brain because the heart does not have to pump blood against gravity. There are many different causes of fainting (see Causes of Fainting in this part), and normally a victim will recover without any problems. Fainting victims can sustain serious injuries when they fall to the floor, especially if they are elderly. Always seek medical attention if you are concerned a victim is injured following a faint.

✚ Causes of Fainting

During an emergency, there can be many things that will cause people to faint. These include:

- Environmental trigger: unpleasant sight or smell or excessive heat
- Medication use
- Dehydration
- Abnormal heartbeat
- Underlying heart problem

✚ Signs and Symptoms of Fainting

- Temporary loss of consciousness followed by a quick recovery
- Feeling weak, light-headed, or sick
- Pale, gray skin
- Sweating
- Presence of an external trigger that caused the faint (for example, the sight of blood from a nosebleed)

✚ First Aid Treatment for Fainting

1. If a victim feels he is going to faint, advise him to lie or sit down as quickly as possible.
2. If he loses consciousness, position the victim on his back and raise his legs to improve blood flow to the brain.
3. The victim should quickly recover. If he does not, ensure the airway is open and he is breathing normally. Prepare to follow CPR steps (including calling EMS) if necessary.
4. Check for any injuries if the victim has fallen.
5. Monitor vital signs and provide reassurance until the faint resolves. If you are concerned that the victim is not recovering quickly, or the victim has sustained an injury, call medical services.

Black Eye

In the midst of a serious emergency, a black eye may seem incidental, but it should be treated as soon as possible. A black eye occurs when there is bruising around the eye. Often, this happens after a direct blow to the face; small blood vessels underneath the skin are damaged and blood collects there, causing swelling and bruising. Black eyes can look serious, but they often start to heal within a few days. You should be aware that a victim with a black eye may also have a head injury or fracture to the face and she may require urgent medical attention for this injury. It is important to check for any injury to the eye itself. If the eye is damaged, specialist medical attention will be required to prevent any permanent damage to the victim's vision.

When to Seek Medical Advice

In the middle of a disaster, medical advice may not be available. However, if it is, consult a medical professional if you are concerned about a black eye, or if any of the following are present:

- Evidence of a serious head injury, such as loss of consciousness, seizures, or vomiting
- Significant swelling around the eye or intense pain
- Bleeding into the eye, or from the ear or nose
- Vision changes
- Inability to move the eyeball
- Evidence of infection such as increasing pain, swelling, or redness
- Use of blood-thinning medication (anticoagulants) by the victim

✚ Basic First Aid Treatments for a Black Eye

1. Assess the victim for any evidence of a serious head injury or damage to the eye.
2. Clean and cover any open cuts or grazes.
3. Apply an ice pack or cold compress to the affected area to reduce the swelling; do not apply ice directly to the skin.

✚ Don't Use Raw Meat

Using raw meat (such as steak) to speed up healing of a black eye is a first aid myth. There is no evidence that meat will aid healing, and it could worsen the situation by introducing infection into the eye. So, save yourself some meat and use a cold compress or ice pack instead!

Broken Nose

Injuries to the nose are common, especially when people are rushing around, as can happen in an emergency. It can sometimes be difficult to tell whether the nose is broken or just badly bruised and swollen. If a broken nose is in the wrong position, it may need realignment by a medical professional. Rarely, a broken nose can lead to more serious damage to the nose or the underlying bones of the face. In some cases, surgery may be required to fix the break. Always seek early medical attention (when that becomes available) for a suspected broken nose. You should be aware that a victim with a broken nose may also have a head injury, and he may require urgent medical attention for this.

✚ Signs and Symptoms of a Broken Nose
- Swelling around the nose
- An obvious deformity
- Pain and tenderness
- A cracking or grating sound when touching the nose
- Bleeding

✚ First Aid Treatment for a Broken Nose
1. Assess the victim for any evidence of a serious head injury.
2. Clean and cover any open cuts or grazes on the nose.
3. Apply an ice pack or cold compress to the affected area to reduce the swelling; do not apply ice directly to the skin.
4. Treat any nosebleeds by asking the victim to lean forward and pinch the soft part of the nose while he breathes through his

mouth for a minimum of ten minutes (see Nosebleeds earlier in this part).

5. Seek medical attention; do not attempt to reposition the nose yourself, as you risk causing further damage.

Minor Burns

Almost half a million Americans each year require hospital treatment due to burn injuries. The majority of burn injuries are minor burns and do not cause any serious complications. In the event of a fire or some other emergency, there is the possibility of both major and minor burns. In this section we'll look at how to effectively treat a minor burn injury. If a victim has suffered major burns, she will need urgent medical treatment (we'll discuss this in **PART 6**). A minor burn normally only affects the superficial layer of the skin. In some cases, a small blister may form over the burn site.

Minor burn injuries can be very painful! Prompt first aid treatment can reduce the pain and swelling from a burn injury and speed the recovery process for the victim. You should be aware that all burn injuries are at high risk of becoming infected. This is because a burn causes a break in the skin, which is our protective barrier against germs. Always seek medical advice if you are concerned a burn is infected, as antibiotics may be required to treat the infection.

+ First Aid Treatment for a Minor Burn
1. Immediately cool the burned area for a minimum of twenty minutes with cool running water.
2. If possible, remove any rings, watches, or straps near the burned area before the area begins to swell.
3. Cover the burn loosely with a nonfluffy sterile dressing from your first aid kit. Clean plastic wrap can be used if no sterile dressings are available.

✛ Common Minor Burn Injury Myths

There are many myths regarding the correct first aid treatment of burns. Many food products have been suggested as potential treatments for burns; however, it's best to keep the butter and mayonnaise in the fridge and use only water to cool a burn.

- Do not apply toothpaste, butter, or any other foodstuff to a burn. This will not cool the burn adequately. The best method to cool a minor burn is by using running water.
- Do not burst blisters; doing this will increase the risk of infection.
- Do not place ice on a minor burn to speed up the cooling process; the ice could make the injury worse by causing freeze burns to the skin.

When to Seek Help

Even minor burns may require specialist medical attention. The following situations always require medical assistance:

- The burn involves the face, feet, hands, or genital area, or the burn area is very large
- There is any evidence of infection in the burn; for example, increasing pain, redness, or discharge of pus
- The burn is located near a joint, such as the knee
- The victim is elderly or a very young child
- Large blisters have formed
- Rings or watches are stuck due to excess swelling around the burn
- The victim's tetanus immunizations are not up-to-date

PART 6

Traumatic Injuries

PART 6

Traumatic Injuries

As well as encountering minor injuries during a major emergency, it's quite possible that you may encounter a victim with more serious injuries, such as severe bleeding or a head injury. Some of these injuries can be life-threatening, and you need to know the correct steps to take if you find yourself looking after an injured victim. The actions you take (for example, applying pressure to a badly bleeding wound) in the first few minutes following a serious traumatic injury could be lifesaving!

When dealing with traumatic injuries, remember to consider your own safety. These can be chaotic and dangerous situations to enter. Always carry out an assessment of the scene and identify potential hazards before rushing in to help. Let's start by looking at how you can help a victim who is bleeding profusely from a major wound.

Severe Bleeding

Our blood is responsible for carrying oxygen through our bodies and delivering it to our vital cells and tissues. Blood also removes waste products from cells and prevents the buildup of toxins. The average adult has around 5 liters of blood, although this depends on weight and size. Blood is transported through the body in three main blood vessels: arteries, veins, and capillaries. Let's take a look at these in more detail and see what happens when they are damaged.

Arteries carry blood under high pressure away from the heart, veins carry blood under low pressure back to the heart, and capillaries are tiny vessels that deliver blood to the cells of the body. Injury to an artery will cause a wound to bleed quickly, since the blood in the artery is under high pressure. These wounds are serious and require urgent first aid steps to stem the bleeding. In some cases, the blood will spurt out of a wound due to the pressure in the artery. The blood in a vein is under less pressure, so blood will not spurt out. However, large veins carry lots of blood, and injuries to these will cause significant bleeding. Injury to the small capillaries causes blood to ooze from a wound; you often see this with small cuts and grazes.

Severe bleeding is an emergency situation, and losing too much blood is life-threatening for the victim. The main concern with severe blood loss is the victim going into shock (see Shock

> **Medical Terminology**
> The medical term for bleeding is *hemorrhage*.

later in this part). Swift first aid treatment is vital to stopping or slowing the bleeding before the arrival of emergency medical help. When dealing with a severe bleeding situation, ensure you are aware of your own safety and take adequate precautions to protect yourself from blood-borne viruses.

✛ First Aid Treatment for a Major Bleed
1. Immediately call EMS.
2. Wear disposable gloves and apply firm, continuous, direct pressure over the bleeding point using sterile dressing if possible or a clean nonfluffy cloth.

3. If the wound is on a limb, elevate the limb above the level of the heart to reduce blood loss.

4. If available, secure a sterile pressure bandage directly over the wound (see Applying a Pressure Bandage to Stop Bleeding in the **APPENDIX**).

5. If direct pressure does not control the bleeding from a limb, or the bleeding is catastrophic, apply a tourniquet above the wound to control bleeding.

6. Monitor for the development of shock (see Shock section later in this part), record vital signs, and provide reassurance until EMS arrives.

The direct pressure needs to be applied over the bleeding point of the wound to be effective. Be aware that a large wound may have more than one active bleeding point.

✦ Using Tourniquets to Stem Bleeding

Evidence has shown that tourniquets are an effective method of stopping life-threatening major bleeding from a limb. They work by cutting off blood supply beyond the tourniquet, thereby stopping blood loss from the wound. If you are trained to do so, consider using a tourniquet in the extreme case of life-threatening bleeding from a limb that can't be controlled by firm direct pressure. Many large first aid kits now contain tourniquets. The tourniquet should be applied approximately 2 inches above the wound but not directly over a joint. Ensure you accurately record the time the tourniquet was applied and hand over this information to EMS.

Leave Embedded Objects

If you notice a foreign object embedded in a wound, do not remove it. This could cause further bleeding or damage to the underlying tissues. Instead, apply pressure around the object in order to stop bleeding, and seek urgent medical attention.

PART 6

Accidental Amputation

An amputation occurs when a limb (or part of a limb) is severed from the body. Amputations can cause significant blood loss, and quick first aid treatment is important to stop severe bleeding and prevent shock. If possible, the amputated body part should be cooled to maximize the chances of surgical reattachment at the hospital. However, it is important not to place the limb in direct contact with ice, as this could damage it. Amputations of fingers and thumbs are often caused by workplace or DIY injuries. Amputations of arms and legs are often seen following an explosion or other high-impact trauma such as a high-speed motor vehicle collision. Witnessing an amputation can be emotionally traumatizing for a rescuer, especially if there are multiple injured victims involved. The priority is to stop severe bleeding to buy the victim time before the arrival of EMS.

✚ First Aid Treatment for an Amputation

1. If possible, immediately call EMS.
2. Treat any severe bleeding (see First Aid Treatment for a Major Bleed in this part), and monitor the victim for shock; you may need to apply a tourniquet (if you have received tourniquet first aid training) to control severe bleeding from an amputated limb.
3. If possible, locate the amputated body part.
4. Wrap the amputated part in a sterile dressing and a clean plastic bag. Place in another larger plastic bag.
5. Place the bags containing the amputated part in a container of ice-cold water if available.

The aim is to keep the amputated part cool to increase the chances of surgical reattachment at the hospital. Remember, do not place the amputated part in direct contact with ice or water, as this could damage the delicate tissues and blood vessels.

Puncture Wounds

A puncture wound occurs when a sharp object pierces the skin. During an emergency such as a hurricane or tornado, it's possible that a flying piece of metal or wood could cause such a wound. Animal bites are another relatively common cause of puncture wounds. Puncture wounds may look minor, and there might not be much bleeding from the wound; however, they can cause serious complications such as infection and damage to underlying nerves and muscles. It is very difficult to assess how deep a puncture wound is, or what damage the object has caused underneath the wound. For this reason, all puncture wounds should be assessed by a medical professional. Many puncture wounds require an X-ray to ensure there are no fragments of the object still embedded in the wound. Surgical removal of any embedded objects may be required to reduce the risk of a serious infection developing and to allow the wound to heal properly.

✚ **First Aid Treatment for a Puncture Wound**
1. Wash your hands thoroughly; use protective gloves if possible.
2. Apply direct pressure with a clean bandage or cloth to stop any bleeding.
3. Call EMS immediately if the wound is to the neck, or if you suspect it is a deep wound to the back, head, scrotum, abdomen, pelvis, chest, or thigh, or over a joint.
4. If there is an object still embedded in the wound, do not remove it; instead, apply padding around the object and seek medical assistance.
5. If the wound has been bleeding heavily, monitor the victim for shock. Call EMS if you are concerned the victim is going into shock or you are unable to stem the bleeding.
6. Try to identify the object that caused the puncture wound.
7. Seek medical help for next steps; the victim may require antibiotic treatment to prevent a serious infection from developing, or advice about tetanus shots or wounds caused by humans or animals.

Shock

You've probably heard the term *shock* used when people talk about an injured victim, but what exactly is shock, and why is it so important to identify in first aid? Shock occurs when our body tissues do not receive an adequate supply of oxygen. Oxygen is vital to allow the tissues in our body to work properly. Without oxygen our cells cannot function and will start to die. This causes damage to the brain and other vital organs.

Severe blood loss is one cause of shock. This makes sense since there is less blood available to carry oxygen through the body to the cells. This is a life-threatening situation and requires urgent medical intervention to replace the blood lost. Major burn injuries can also cause shock, as burns cause fluid to leak into the injury (see Major Burns later in this part), and therefore, there is less fluid flowing through the body for the rest of the cells. A victim suffering from anaphylaxis (a major allergic reaction) may also go into shock. There are other causes of shock besides these examples.

You need to be aware of the signs and symptoms of shock and constantly monitor a victim for the warning signs that may indicate shock. The shock we've described here is different from mental or psychological shock following a distressing event. People who witness a traumatic event are often described as being "in shock," but this is not the same as physical shock caused by excessive blood loss.

Here are some of the signs and symptoms of shock:

- Pale, cold, or clammy skin
- Increased pulse and respiratory rate
- Weak pulse that is difficult to find
- Nausea or vomiting
- Changes in behavior
- Reduced level of consciousness (late sign)

✚ First Aid Treatment for Shock

1. Immediately call 911.
2. Find and treat the cause of the shock (for example, by stopping any serious bleeding).
3. Lay the victim down, and elevate the legs 6–12 inches unless this may cause further injury (for example, leg or pelvic [hip] injury).
4. Keep the victim warm, and do not give him anything to eat or drink.
5. Provide reassurance and monitor vital signs. Prepare to perform CPR if necessary.

Your priority in first aid is to identify shock in a victim and stop it from worsening. You cannot replace the blood lost by a victim, but effective first aid can stop further blood loss and prevent the shock from worsening. In addition, rapid treatment of burns and anaphylaxis can also help prevent shock.

Fractures (Closed)

Fractures (or broken bones) are common injuries among children and adults, and many of us will break at least one bone in our lifetime. It's not uncommon for them to occur during a serious emergency. A fracture occurs when excessive force is applied to a bone, resulting in the bone breaking. Simple trips and falls cause the majority of fractures, especially to the arm and wrist. Athletics and adventure sports are common causes of broken legs and ankles. Sometimes it can be difficult to tell the difference between a fracture and a soft-tissue injury (sprain or strain); there have been many cases of people walking around for several days on a broken ankle before seeking help! An X-ray is required to tell if a bone is broken, so always seek medical attention if you are concerned that a victim may have fractured a bone.

Let's look at the main types of fractures you might encounter in an emergency situation.

A closed fracture occurs when a bone is broken but does not cause a break in the skin. The majority of fractures are closed. If the bone does cut through the skin, this is known as an open fracture. Any wound overlying a fracture should be suspected to be caused by an open fracture. We'll take a closer look at open fractures in the next section.

Complicated fractures occur when the broken bone damages blood vessels or nerves near the fracture site. These fractures require urgent specialist medical treatment to reduce the risk of long-term complications such as permanent nerve damage.

Fractures may occur alongside a dislocation (for example, a dislocated shoulder can also be broken). Fractures can be very painful for a victim, especially if the limb is badly broken. Your main aim in first aid is to prevent excessive movement of the fracture to reduce pain and any internal bleeding. All fracture victims require an X-ray and assessment by a medical professional. Some fractures may require realignment in the hospital and, in some cases, surgery to fix the broken bone.

> **Medical Terminology**
>
> The medical term for a broken bone is *fracture*. These two terms mean the same thing.

Here are some of the signs and symptoms of a fracture. They can be remembered by using the acronym PLASTIC. It is easier to assess for angulation or irregularity in a limb by comparing the suspected fracture to the other unaffected side.

- **P**ain
- **L**oss of movement
- **A**ngulation (abnormal bend or curve) of the limb
- **S**welling
- **T**enderness
- **I**rregularity
- **C**repitus (a cracking or grating sound)

✛ First Aid Treatment for a Fracture

1. Treat any severe bleeding.
2. Stabilize the injury to prevent movement of the fracture.
3. If the fracture is open, apply a sterile dressing over the wound to reduce the risk of infection.
4. Apply ice packs to the wound.
5. Check for signs of circulation beyond the fracture (see Checking for Circulation in this part); if circulation beyond the injury appears to be damaged, seek urgent medical assistance.
6. Monitor the victim for shock and record vital signs (see sidebar, Watch Out for Shock).
7. Seek medical assistance or call EMS.

> **Watch Out for Shock**
>
> A fracture of a large bone, such as the femur or pelvis, can cause significant internal bleeding. The victim may lose so much blood that she starts to go into shock (see Shock earlier in this part). Always monitor a victim with a suspected major fracture for shock.

✛ Checking for Circulation

A complicated fracture may damage the circulation in a limb. This is an emergency and could lead to permanent paralysis or, at worst, require amputation. Signs of compromised circulation include the limb turning pale or blue or feeling cold to the touch. The victim may complain of numbness in the limb and be unable to move the affected area.

✛ First Aid Treatment for a Fractured Arm

1. Follow the general first aid steps for a fracture (see First Aid Treatment for a Fracture earlier in this part).
2. Pad around the injury, and support above and below the fracture using your hands.
3. Place the affected arm in an arm sling (see Making a Sling for a Broken Arm in the **APPENDIX**).

PART 6

4. If no sling is available, ask the victim to support the arm in the most comfortable position; take caution to avoid any excessive movement of the injured arm.

5. Seek medical attention; the victim will require an X-ray to assess the injury and decide on the correct ongoing treatment.

+ First Aid Treatment for a Fractured Leg

1. Follow the general first aid steps for a fracture (see First Aid Treatment for a Fracture earlier in this part).

2. Pad around the injury, and support above and below the fracture using your hands or by applying a splint if trained.

3. Call medical services.

4. Do not allow the victim to walk or put weight on the injury.

5. Do not attempt to realign or straighten the leg.

Fractures (Open)

Open fractures occur when there is a wound caused by a broken bone piercing the skin.

Open fractures are more severe than closed fractures, as there is a significant risk of infection in the exposed bone; this can lead to widespread infection or even the loss of a limb. Thankfully, open fractures are relatively rare, as they require a lot of force to occur. However, that a fracture is open sometimes can go unnoticed; the bone may not always be visible in the wound. After an injury, the muscles around a fracture go into spasm, and this can pull the exposed bone back underneath the skin. For this reason, you should assume any wound overlying a fracture is caused by an open fracture until proven otherwise.

> **Medical Terminology**
>
> The medical term for an open fracture is *compound fracture*.

Your main aim in first aid when dealing with an open fracture is to control any life-threatening bleeding and reduce the risk of infection.

PART 6

If possible, do not place pressure on a protruding bone. A tourniquet may be needed if the fracture severed an artery. Place a sterile dressing over the wound or exposed bone as soon as possible to reduce the risk of the bone becoming contaminated. Open fractures are painful, and the victim is likely to be very distressed with the injury, so remain calm and provide reassurance until medical help arrives. All open fractures normally require surgery to thoroughly clean the injury and the administration of strong antibiotics to prevent a severe bone infection from developing.

✚ First Aid Treatment for an Open Fracture

1. Call EMS.
2. Treat any severe bleeding; an open fracture can cause severe bleeding if the broken bone has damaged a large blood vessel.
3. Stabilize the injury to prevent movement of the fracture; further movement could worsen any bleeding.
4. Apply a sterile dressing over the wound to reduce the risk of infection.
5. Monitor the victim for shock and record vital signs until EMS arrives.

Dislocations

A dislocation occurs when a bone moves out of the correct position at a joint. These injuries can be very painful, as anyone who has experienced a dislocated joint will know! Common sites for dislocations include the shoulder, elbow, and fingers. A common cause of a dislocated joint is excessive force being applied to the joint (for example, following a fall). A dislocation injury may be accompanied by a fracture, and it is difficult to assess for a fracture. Therefore, most victims require an X-ray before attempting to reduce the bone back into the joint. (The term *reduce* is used to describe the act of bringing parts back to their normal positions.) It is important that you do not attempt to relocate, or reduce, a dislocated joint; the victim requires assessment by a medical professional. Otherwise, you risk causing further permanent damage to the bone, nerves, or blood vessels. Your main aim is to support the joint in the position found and prevent further movement of the injured area.

A dislocation injury may cause damage to the ligaments that support a joint. This can make the joint unstable and the victim more prone to recurrent dislocations. Physical therapy or, in some cases, surgery may be required to fix and strengthen the ligaments to prevent dislocations from occurring. A victim who has suffered a dislocation injury should seek advice from a medical professional or physiotherapist before returning to any athletic activity, especially contact sports.

✚ Signs and Symptoms of a Dislocation

The signs and symptoms of a dislocation are similar to those of a fracture:

- Pain
- Loss of movement
- Angulation of the limb
- Swelling
- Tenderness
- Irregularity
- Crepitus (a cracking or grating sound)

> **Shoulder Dislocation Following a Seizure**
>
> A victim having a major seizure is at risk of a shoulder dislocation due to excessive muscle contractions. Do not attempt to restrain a victim having a seizure in order to prevent a dislocation. You are likely to cause injury to yourself or the victim and worsen the situation.

The abnormal angulation of a limb may be more prominent in a dislocation injury. You should compare the affected limb with the unaffected side of the body to assess for angulation and irregularity.

✚ First Aid Treatment for a Dislocated Joint
1. Support the limb in the position found; do not attempt to reduce the dislocation.

2. Apply padding around the injury.
3. Check for signs of circulation beyond the injury.
4. If the victim has dislocated his shoulder, elbow, or wrist, then an arm sling may be useful to support the injury.
5. Seek medical assistance or call EMS. Monitor the victim for shock and record vital signs.

Crush Injuries

Major crush injuries are life-threatening situations and will require early specialist help to safely extricate and treat the victim. A major crush injury occurs when a large part of the body (for example, the chest) is crushed. An example of this is a victim trapped underneath a car following a motor vehicle collision. These victims often have multiple injuries and require advanced medical help at the scene of the incident, so never delay in calling for EMS. Minor crush injuries, such as fingers or toes, often occur in the workplace or at home when performing DIY projects. A crush injury can be complicated by bleeding or a fracture of the bones underneath the skin.

You need to be aware that victims of major crush injuries are at risk of developing crush syndrome. This syndrome occurs when a major crush injury causes the buildup of toxins in the damaged tissue. When the object causing the crush is removed, and pressure on the injury is released, these toxins spread through the body and can cause fatal heart abnormalities and kidney damage. As a result, a major crush injury victim can quickly deteriorate after the crushing object has been removed.

✚ **First Aid Treatment for a Major Crush Injury**
1. Ensure the scene is safe for you to approach.
2. Call EMS.
3. Look for and treat any severe bleeding found.
4. Monitor for shock, monitor vital signs, and provide reassurance until the arrival of EMS.

PART 6

If the victim has been trapped for a long time, releasing pressure may lead to the development of crush syndrome, and the victim may quickly deteriorate. If a victim has been trapped for a prolonged period, communicate with the EMS operator and seek expert advice.

Head Injuries

Head injuries can range from minor bumps to life-threatening head trauma. Our brains are made up of a delicate network of cells and pathways that enable us to think and control our bodies. The skull is responsible for protecting our brain from knocks and bumps. Minor head injuries often cause *concussions*. What exactly does this term mean?

A concussion occurs when the brain is shaken in the skull, causing a temporary disturbance in brain functioning. However, any head injury carries the risk of bleeding or swelling inside the brain. This situation is life-threatening; because the skull is a fixed box, it does not allow the brain to bulge outward or swell. Therefore, any swelling or bleeding in the brain will rapidly increase the pressure inside the skull and cause the delicate brain cells and networks to be compressed. This situation can develop rapidly and lead to life-threatening and life-changing brain damage. The symptoms of a severe head injury may be delayed by several hours after the initial injury, as the pressure in the skull can take time to build up. As a result, all head injury victims should be evaluated by a trained medical professional.

In addition to injuries to the brain, the bones of the skull can be fractured following a direct blow to the head. Skull fractures can bleed significantly, and they expose the delicate brain tissue to the outside environment, so there is a risk of infection. These injuries often require the victim to undergo surgery to fix the fracture and strong antibiotics to prevent brain infection.

Any victim with a serious head injury is presumed to have a neck injury (see Neck and Back Injuries later in this part) until evaluated by a medical professional. The head is connected to the body via the spine;

therefore, blows to the head can put stress on the neck and risk causing a spinal injury.

✚ Signs and Symptoms of Concussion
- A brief loss of consciousness
- Headache
- Memory loss of the incident
- Nausea
- Dizziness
- Visual disturbance (for example, blurred or double vision)

These are signs and symptoms of a life-threatening head injury:

- A temporary improvement in consciousness, followed by decreasing responsiveness
- Vomiting
- One pupil larger than the other
- Evidence of a skull fracture or severe bleeding from a head wound
- Seizures
- Blood or fluid leaking from the nose or ears
- Severe memory loss of events before or after the head injury

✚ First Aid Treatment for a Major Head Injury
1. Call EMS.
2. Treat any severe bleeding from the head by applying direct pressure.
3. Support the victim's head and neck in the position found; avoid excessive movement of the victim.
4. Monitor vital signs and level of consciousness.
5. If the victim becomes unconscious and her airway is blocked, she will need to be carefully placed in the recovery position to protect the airway.
6. Be prepared to perform CPR if the victim stops breathing normally (see How to Perform CPR in **PART 5**).

+ Monitoring Level of Consciousness Using AVPU

Following a head injury, a victim may have a reduced level of consciousness. To assess this, you can use the AVPU scale:

- **A**lert: The victim is alert and conversing with you
- **V**oice: The victim only responds to verbal instructions
- **P**ain: The victim only responds to a pain stimulus (for example, pinching the top of the shoulder)
- **U**nconscious: The victim does not respond to a verbal or pain stimulus

Any victim who has had a head injury, however minor, while taking blood-thinning medication must seek urgent medical help, as he may require a scan of his brain to check for internal bleeding.

Neck and Back Injuries

In many emergency conditions, neck and back injuries are common: You're hurrying, carrying heavy objects, and so on. It's important to be careful, but if you or someone else in your immediate vicinity is injured in this way, you should know what to do.

The spine is the major structure in the neck and back, but what exactly makes up our spines? Our spines are composed of individual bones that form a tunnel stretching from the top of the neck to the lower back. Through this tunnel runs the spinal cord, a complex network of nerves and cells, which sends signals to and from the brain. The spinal cord is responsible for transmitting sensory information to the brain (for example, the sensation of pain) and for conveying commands from the brain to the muscles (for example, to move your arm). As well as carrying the spinal cord, the bones of

Medical Terminology

The individual bones that make up the spine are called *vertebrae*.

the spine support the body and provide an attachment for many muscles that give us flexibility and strength.

Excessive force applied to the back or neck can fracture the bones that make up the spine and cause permanent damage to the spinal cord. This force could be from a direct blow or a trauma situation such as a fall from height or a high-speed motor vehicle collision. Spinal cord injury can cause permanent paralysis of limbs and a loss of sensation. This is a serious, life-changing injury for the victim and often requires a long period of rehabilitation.

How can you help a victim with a suspected neck or back injury? The key is to minimize any movement of the victim following the injury. Further movement following an injury to the spine can cause more damage to the spinal cord and worsen the injury. Therefore, your priority is to keep the victim as still as possible before the arrival of EMS. Remember, preventing worsening of the victim's condition is one of the key aims in any first aid situation.

✦ When to Suspect a Neck or Back Injury

You should suspect that a victim may have sustained a neck or back injury in the following situations:

- Fall from height or falling awkwardly
- Car or motorbike accident
- Head injury with reduced level of consciousness
- Direct blow to the neck or back
- Head injury from diving into a shallow pool
- Sports injury
- Horseback-riding accident (for example, being thrown from a horse)
- Multiple traumatic injuries
- An injured victim under the influence of alcohol or drugs

Here are some of the signs and symptoms of a neck or back injury:

- Neck or back pain
- Evidence of a serious head injury
- Loss of (or weak) movement of arms or legs
- Altered sensation in arms or legs (numbness, burning, or tingling sensations)
- Loss of control of bladder or bowels
- Difficulty breathing

✛ First Aid Treatment for a Neck or Back Injury (Victim Is Awake)

If the victim is awake, then you should:

1. Call EMS.
2. Keep the victim supported (outlined in the following steps) in the position found; avoid any movement of the head, neck, or back.
3. Kneel or lie down above the victim's head and place your hands on both sides of his head to keep the neck still; do not attempt to realign the neck.
4. If available, place rolled-up blankets or towels on either side of the head to minimize movement of the neck.
5. Monitor vital signs and level of consciousness until EMS arrives.

✛ First Aid Treatment for a Neck or Back Injury (Victim Is Unresponsive)

If the victim is unresponsive, then you should follow the DR ABC action plan described in **PART 5**, but with some modifications. Check that the situation is safe to approach and the victim is unresponsive. Ensure EMS has been called. Then:

1. Open the airway using the jaw-thrust technique:
    1. Kneel above the victim's head.
    2. Place your hands on each side of his head with your thumbs over his cheekbones and fingertips at the angles of the jaw.

PART 6: Traumatic Injuries

3. Using your fingers, lift the jaw forward, but do not tilt the head backward.
2. Check for the presence of normal breathing.
3. If the victim is not breathing, immediately update EMS and commence CPR (see How to Perform CPR in **PART 5**).
4. If the victim is breathing normally, try to support him in the position found and maintain his airway with a jaw thrust.
5. If the victim is breathing normally but he is vomiting or his airway is obstructed, then he will need to be placed in the recovery position to protect his airway (see sidebar, Using the Recovery Position).

Major Burns

Whether you're in a house fire or a forest fire, burns are serious injuries that need the right treatment. As previously mentioned, almost half a million Americans each year require hospital treatment due to burn injuries. Major burn injuries can be life-threatening and life-changing because of the risk of permanent scarring. You can really make a difference to a burn injury victim by providing early effective first aid treatment for the burn and by calling for EMS early.

Why is early first aid treatment vital for burn injury victims? The burning process continues even after the cause of the burn has been

Using the Recovery Position

A victim with a suspected neck or back injury should be moved as little as possible in order to protect his spine. Ideally, he should be left in the position in which he is found. However, if the victim is on his back and you are unable to keep his airway open (for example, because he is vomiting), then he is at risk of choking. You will need to carefully turn the victim onto his side, ideally with another person supporting the head and neck in line with the rest of the body, using the technique described earlier (see Recovery Position in **PART 5**). If more helpers are available, they can support the back and neck to minimize movement of the spine as the victim rolls over.

removed. This causes further damage to the skin and underlying tissues. Cooling with running water will remove heat from the burn and prevent further damage from occurring. (Note that this is applicable for minor burns in which the skin isn't broken.) Burns that are cooled quickly will heal faster and with fewer complications such as long-term scarring. When cooling a burn, you always need to be aware of the risk of hypothermia setting in, especially in children. Try to keep the victim warm while cooling the affected area (see sidebar, Warm the Victim).

Burn injuries can be classified into three different depths. Most burns are due to contact with a hot surface or liquid, which causes damage to the skin and underlying tissues. However, there are other causes of burns including chemicals and the sun. We'll cover the latter type of burn in **PART 7**.

You need to watch out for shock in a burn victim. Major burns cause significant loss of fluid through the damaged skin, which can cause shock. Always monitor a major burn victim for signs and symptoms of shock.

✚ Burn Injury Depths
Burn injuries can be broadly divided into three different depths:

- Superficial (first degree): damage to the top layer of skin cells
- Partial thickness (second degree): blistering of the skin
- Full thickness (third degree): damage to deep muscle and soft tissues

You may find a burn injury has areas of different depths. For example, a severe burn may be third degree in the center with areas of second- and first-degree burns surrounding it.

✛ First Aid Treatment for Major Burns

1. Call EMS.
2. If the burn is affecting a limb, carefully remove any rings, watches, or straps near the burned area.
3. Cover the burn loosely with a nonfluffy sterile dressing. Clean plastic wrap can be used if no sterile dressings are available.
4. Monitor the victim for hypothermia (see sidebar, Warm the Victim) and shock.

Major burn injuries can be life-threatening, especially in children and the elderly. Always call EMS for a major burn victim. In addition, infection is a common complication following burns, and these injuries need careful assessment and management by a specialist burn center.

✛ Common Major Burn Injury Myths

There are many myths regarding the first aid treatment of burns.

- Do not apply toothpaste or butter to a burn. This will not cool the burn adequately and may cause further damage. The best method to cool a major burn is to run cool water over it.
- Do not burst blisters, as this will increase the risk of infection.
- Do not remove clothing stuck to burned skin. This can cause further damage to the skin.

> **Warm the Victim**
>
> You need to keep her warm. For example, blankets can be used to cover unburned areas. It is important to prevent hypothermia, since low body temperature can cause further complications for victims with major burns.

PART 6

Chemical Burns

Strong chemicals can cause burns to the skin and underlying tissues. Although they are less common than heat burns, chemical burns can cause major injury to a victim and may be associated with the production of toxic fumes. You must always consider your own safety before entering a potentially hazardous situation involving chemicals. Remember, you are the most important person in any emergency situation!

Chemical burns may occur in the event of a chemical spill. If this happens, your main aim in first aid is to flush the chemical responsible for causing the burn off the skin to reduce ongoing burning. This will require lots of running water (for example, from a garden hose). The waste runoff water should be treated as potentially contaminated with chemicals. Make sure the runoff water is directed away from you and the victim.

✚ First Aid Treatment for Chemical Burns

1. Ensure the scene is safe for you to approach; be aware of the risk of toxic fumes from chemicals.
2. Immediately call EMS, and tell the emergency operator that the victim has come into contact with dangerous chemicals.
3. Put on protective gloves.
4. Flood the burned area with running water for at least twenty minutes, ensuring the runoff wastewater is directed away from the victim and you.
5. Carefully remove contaminated clothing if safe to do so.
6. Try to identify the substance that caused the burn, and hand over this information to EMS when they arrive.

✚ Which Burns *Not* to Flood with Water

Chemical burns caused by contact with elemental metals (for example, magnesium, lithium, sodium, potassium, and phosphorus) or dry lime should not be flooded with water, as contact with water will cause a chemical reaction on the victim's skin. If a powder is visible on the skin, it should be brushed off as quickly as possible. For dry lime, after the powder is brushed off, the burn area should be flooded with water.

✚ Chemical Burns to the Eye

Strong chemicals splashing into the eye can cause permanent damage to the eye and loss of sight. If a victim has chemicals in his eye, irrigate the eye for at least twenty minutes (see Irrigating an Eye to Remove a Foreign Body in the **APPENDIX**) and seek urgent medical attention. Do not attempt to neutralize the chemical by putting other substances into the eye; this could cause further harm.

PART 7

Medical Emergencies

PART 7

PART 7

Medical Emergencies

Being able to spot the warning signs of a serious medical emergency is an important skill in first aid. The victim may not always appreciate the seriousness of the symptoms she is experiencing, so it is your role to recognize the important warning signs and summon early medical help. You can also make a difference and potentially save a life by administering early treatment. You also need to know what *not* to do. Unfortunately, there are many myths circulating about treating medical conditions, such as seizures. Some of these incorrect beliefs could make the situation much worse and cause harm to the victim. In this part, we'll guide you through some of the most serious medical emergencies and how to recognize them and start early treatment; we'll also debunk some of the most common first aid myths. Let's start by looking at heart attacks, one of the most serious medical emergencies you may encounter.

Heart Attack

The heart is a muscular pump responsible for moving blood through the body. Our hearts need an excellent blood supply to provide enough oxygen to keep the heart muscle pumping effectively. A heart attack occurs when the blood supply to the heart is interrupted, leading to part of the heart muscle being injured or dying. This is different from a cardiac arrest.

Why does a heart attack happen? The blood vessels that supply the heart are called the coronary arteries. As we age, our coronary arteries can become lined with plaque, which contains cholesterol and other fatty substances that build up in the wall of the artery. Lifestyle factors including smoking, obesity, and an unhealthy diet all accelerate this process.

Medical Terminology

The medical term for a heart attack is *myocardial infarction*. The term *myocardial* refers to the heart muscle, and *infarction* means the death of tissue due to lack of oxygen.

The terms *heart attack* and *cardiac arrest* are commonly confused, especially in the media. A heart attack is a medical condition caused by the blockage of a blood vessel supplying the heart. A cardiac arrest occurs when the heart stops pumping blood through the body, so the victim loses consciousness and stops breathing. A heart attack may cause a cardiac arrest, but there are many other causes of cardiac arrest.

Over time, the fatty buildup in the lining of the artery increases. Eventually, this fatty buildup can rupture, resulting in the formation of a blood clot. This blood clot blocks the artery and stops blood from flowing to the vital heart muscle. The heart muscle becomes starved of oxygen and starts to die. This causes the victim to experience the common signs and symptoms of a heart attack.

A heart attack requires emergency medical treatment to unblock the artery and restore blood flow to the affected muscle. You must not delay in calling EMS if you suspect a victim is having a heart attack. The quicker the blockage in the artery is cleared, the more likely it is that the heart muscle will make a complete recovery.

Here are some of the signs and symptoms of a heart attack:

- Chest pain or discomfort
- Pain or discomfort in the jaw, back, neck, arms, shoulders, or stomach
- Shortness of breath
- Excessive sweating
- Increased pulse and respiratory rate
- Pale skin
- Nausea and/or vomiting
- Light-headedness

The pain from a heart attack can vary. The classic description is central crushing chest pain. However, any sensation of pain or pressure in the chest should be considered as coming from the heart until proven otherwise.

✦ Watch Out for Silent Heart Attacks

Some heart attacks may not present with the typical symptoms of chest pain radiating to the arm. In rare cases, a victim may have no pain at all. Women and people with diabetes are more likely to experience these "silent" heart attacks. Victims who have a silent heart attack may only have mild pain mistaken for heartburn or a pulled muscle. In some cases, the victim has no symptoms at all.

✦ First Aid Treatment for a Heart Attack

If you suspect a victim may be having a heart attack, you should:

1. Immediately call EMS.
2. Place the victim in a comfortable seated position and loosen any tight clothing.

PART 7

3. Offer to administer a regular-strength (325 milligrams) aspirin tablet if appropriate (see Administering Aspirin to a Heart Attack Victim in this part). Patients should always take medicine as prescribed.
4. Be prepared to perform CPR if the victim loses consciousness and stops breathing (see How to Perform CPR in **PART 5**).
5. Provide reassurance and monitor vital signs until emergency medical help arrives.

✚ Administering Aspirin to a Heart Attack Victim

Early administration of aspirin has been shown to improve the chances of survival from a heart attack. Aspirin helps break down the clot in the blocked blood vessel.

- The aspirin tablet should be chewed and swallowed by the victim.
- Do not administer aspirin if the victim has a known aspirin allergy or a history of recent bleeding.

If you are concerned about administering aspirin, seek advice from EMS over the telephone or await the arrival of expert medical help. Most first aid kits contain emergency aspirin for use in a heart attack situation.

Stroke (Brain Attack)

Our brain cells require a constant supply of oxygen and nutrients to function effectively. A stroke occurs when the blood supply to the brain is interrupted. This interruption in blood supply causes brain cells to die and can result in permanent brain damage. Stroke victims require emergency medical treatment to restore blood flow to the damaged brain tissue. There are two types of stroke; let's take a look at these in more detail.

The most common type of stroke is caused by a blood clot in the blood vessels supplying the brain. The blood clot blocks the vessel, leading to the brain cells being starved of oxygen and nutrients, eventually causing cell death. This is known as an ischemic stroke.

The second type of stroke is caused by a bleed into the brain from a ruptured blood vessel, leading to brain swelling and cell death. This type of stroke is known as a hemorrhagic stroke. Hemorrhagic strokes are much less common than ischemic strokes and are more common in people who take blood-thinning medication.

The treatment for an ischemic stroke is similar to the treatment for a heart attack. The affected blood vessel needs to be unblocked to restore blood flow to the damaged brain tissue. The faster this happens, the more likely the brain cells are to recover and the less likely there will be permanent brain damage. Victims need to have the blood flow restored within three hours to save vital brain tissue and have the best chance of making a good recovery. Therefore, you must not delay in calling EMS if you suspect a victim is having a stroke.

> **Medical Terminology**
>
> The medical term for a stroke is *cerebrovascular event* (CVE) or *cerebrovascular accident* (CVA). The medical term *hemorrhagic* refers to bleeding.

Strokes are now also known as brain attacks, which emphasizes the importance of calling for help early, as you do when you are dealing with a suspected heart attack.

Here are some of the signs and symptoms of a stroke:

- Facial droop on one side
- Numbness, weakness, or paralysis of the face, arm, or leg, especially down one side of the body
- Confusion, trouble speaking, or difficulty understanding others
- Sudden trouble in seeing
- Problems with dizziness, walking, coordination, or balance
- Reduced level of consciousness
- Seizures
- Sudden severe headache

The most common symptoms of a stroke can be remembered by using the acronym FAST.

- **F**ace: Is there any facial droop?
- **A**rms: Can the victim raise both arms?
- **S**peech: Is there any slurred speech?
- **T**ime: Time to call EMS if any one of these symptoms is present.

✦ First Aid Treatment for a Stroke

If you suspect someone may be having a stroke, you should:

1. Immediately call EMS.
2. Place the victim in a comfortable position.
3. Record the time of onset of the symptoms and inform EMS.
4. Provide reassurance and monitor vital signs until emergency medical help arrives.
5. Do not give the victim anything to eat or drink, as there is a risk of choking.

Never administer aspirin to a stroke victim. There is no way in first aid to distinguish between a stroke caused by a bleed (hemorrhagic) or one caused by a clot (ischemic). Administering aspirin will worsen a stroke caused by a bleeding blood vessel.

✦ Watch Out for Ministrokes

A ministroke occurs when the symptoms of a stroke resolve within twenty-four hours with no medical treatment. The medical term for this is *transient ischemic attack* (TIA). A ministroke often occurs before a major stroke, so a TIA should be treated as a serious warning sign. You cannot distinguish a ministroke from a regular stroke; therefore, always call EMS if a victim shows any of the signs and symptoms of a stroke. Do not wait to see if the symptoms resolve on their own before seeking medical assistance.

Asthma

Most of us know someone who is living with asthma. Asthma is a common long-term condition that affects the small air passages in the lungs. During an asthma attack, these small air passages become swollen and blocked with phlegm. This narrows the air passages and restricts airflow through the lungs, which causes the person with asthma to experience difficulty in breathing and often creates a characteristic wheezing noise. Wheezing is a high-pitched whistling noise caused by air trying to flow through the swollen air passages. Why does this swelling happen?

People often develop asthma in childhood. The air passages become sensitive to inhaled particles and environmental changes. These are known as asthma triggers. Common triggers include pollen, air pollution, changes in air temperature, and exercise. When the body comes into contact with a trigger, it responds by releasing chemicals into the air passages, which cause swelling and the production of excessive mucus (phlegm). This causes that person to experience the signs and symptoms of an asthma attack.

Even with modern medical advances, asthma can still be life-threatening, and there are still deaths every year from acute asthma attacks. Someone having an asthma attack can get worse very quickly, so you should always seek medical advice if you are concerned about his breathing.

Here are some of the signs and symptoms of an asthma attack:

- Difficulty in breathing
- A wheezing sound
- A sensation of chest tightness
- Persistent coughing
- Increased respiratory and pulse rate

During severe attacks, the victim may become exhausted and have a decreased level of consciousness. His skin may also turn pale and have a blue tinge around the mouth, ears, or fingernails. These features indicate life-threatening asthma, and emergency medical help is urgently required.

PART 7

✚ First Aid Treatment for an Asthma Attack

If you suspect someone is having an asthma attack you should:

1. Assist the victim in using his inhaled asthma medication.
2. Provide reassurance and monitor vital signs.
3. Immediately call for EMS if:
   1. There is no improvement in symptoms after using his inhaler.
   2. The person is not carrying any medication.
   3. You are worried about the severity of the asthma attack.

Do not delay in calling EMS if you are concerned about someone having an asthma attack. Life-threatening asthma can develop over minutes and requires immediate emergency medical treatment. If in doubt, call for professional medical help.

Anaphylaxis (Severe Allergic Reaction)

During an emergency situation, it's possible that members of your family may be brought into contact with substances to which they're allergic. The result could be the reaction known as anaphylaxis. This is a severe, life-threatening allergic reaction affecting the entire body. Many of us know someone at risk of anaphylaxis, as the condition is becoming more common. Anaphylaxis occurs when the body becomes overly sensitive to a certain trigger. Common triggers of anaphylaxis include food products (nuts, shellfish, fish), insect venom (bees, wasps, ants), medications (antibiotics), and latex. How do these substances cause anaphylaxis?

When the body comes into contact with a trigger, it reacts by releasing large amounts of histamine. In small quantities, histamine is responsible for causing the signs of a mild allergic reaction such as itching or minor swelling. However, when the body releases a massive amount of histamine, it causes a whole-body reaction. This severe reaction is life-threatening, as it causes swelling of the throat and can rapidly obstruct breathing.

The initial emergency treatment of anaphylaxis involves the rapid administration of the drug epinephrine. Epinephrine works to combat the effects of the histamine and reduces the life-threatening swelling. Because anaphylaxis can be fatal in minutes, patients are prescribed epinephrine auto-injector devices for self-administration before the arrival of emergency medical help. Your role is to summon emergency medical assistance and help the victim to use her prescribed auto-injector device.

Signs and symptoms of anaphylaxis include:

- Skin reactions, such as hives (red itchy bumps appearing on the skin), itching, peeling, or flushed, pale skin
- Swelling of the face, tongue, lips, or throat
- Difficulty in breathing
- Dizziness or fainting
- Increased pulse and respiratory rate
- Nausea and vomiting
- Abdominal pain
- Low blood pressure

The signs and symptoms of anaphylaxis can develop rapidly over the minutes following contact with the trigger.

Epinephrine Auto-Injectors

People with a known severe allergy should carry a prescribed epinephrine auto-injector at all times. These devices are designed to inject epinephrine into the thigh muscle during an anaphylaxis episode. There are a variety of brand names, but the most common brand is EpiPen. Auto-injectors have clear instructions on how to use them on the packaging or printed on the devices themselves.

+ **First Aid Treatment for Anaphylaxis**
    1. Immediately call EMS.
    2. If possible, remove the trigger of the anaphylaxis episode.
    3. Assist the person in using her prescribed epinephrine auto-injector (see sidebar, Epinephrine Auto-Injectors) according to label instructions.

PART 7

4. Lay the victim down unless she is having significant breathing problems.
5. Be prepared to perform CPR if the victim loses consciousness and stops breathing (see How to Perform CPR in **PART 5**).
6. Provide reassurance and monitor vital signs until emergency medical help arrives.

Rapid use of an auto-injector may resolve the victim's symptoms. However, medical help must still be sought, as there is a risk of a second delayed reaction.

Meningitis

Meningitis is a serious infection that affects the brain and spinal cord. The main risk from meningitis is that the infection can spread to the bloodstream and be fatal within hours. Why does meningitis occur? Our brains and spinal cords are covered by layers of protective membranes known as meninges. These membranes protect the delicate cells that make up the brain and spinal cord. A variety of bacteria and viruses can infect the meninges and cause inflammation; this is called meningitis. The infection can then spread to the victim's bloodstream and cause blood poisoning (septicemia). This causes the characteristic rash associated with meningitis, which doesn't go away when it is pressed on. Septicemia is life-threatening and requires urgent treatment in the hospital to combat the infection.

Anyone is at risk of catching meningitis. However, children and young people are the most vulnerable, along with people with certain medical conditions. Babies under the age of one year have the highest

Medical Terminology

When an infection spreads to the bloodstream, this is known as *septicemia*.

risk of developing meningitis. Vaccinations play an important role in reducing the risk of meningitis in babies and children, and the number of cases of meningitis has been decreasing. However, vaccinations do not protect against every virus that can cause meningitis. The treatment of meningitis and septicemia involves the rapid administration of strong antibiotics to combat the infection. Delays in administering antibiotics can be fatal; therefore, if you suspect meningitis, do not delay in calling for emergency medical help.

If you come into close contact with a person who may be suffering from meningitis, then you should also seek medical assistance. In some cases, doctors will prescribe antibiotics to protect you from developing the disease.

Some signs and symptoms of meningitis include:

- Headache
- High temperature (fever)
- Neck stiffness
- Sensitivity to light (photophobia)
- Vomiting or upset stomach
- Lethargy
- Loss of appetite
- Reduced level of consciousness
- Seizures
- Confusion

Newborns and infants can have different signs and symptoms:

- High fever
- Constant crying
- Excessive sleepiness or irritability
- Inactivity or sluggishness
- Poor feeding
- A bulge in the soft spot on top of a baby's head (fontanel)
- Stiffness in a baby's body and neck

As the infection spreads to the bloodstream, victims may become drowsy or confused or have a seizure. There may be elevated pulse and respiratory rates. In late stages, a rash may develop, which does not go away when it is pressed on. This is called a non-blanching rash and is a sign of severe blood poisoning (septicemia). Blood poisoning does not always cause a rash, so you must not wait for a rash to develop before calling for help.

✛ First Aid Treatment for Meningitis
1. Immediately call EMS if you are concerned about the possibility of meningitis.
2. Provide reassurance and monitor vital signs until emergency medical help arrives.

There is no effective first aid treatment for meningitis. The victim will require early advanced medical care. Your role is to spot the warning signs that could indicate meningitis and seek early medical help without delay.

✛ Don't Wait for a Rash
You *must not* wait for the development of a rash before calling for medical help. Some patients with severe blood poisoning may not develop a rash at all. If a rash does develop, the tumbler test can be used to determine whether the rash is suggestive of blood poisoning: If the rash does not fade when a glass tumbler is pressed against it, this indicates blood poisoning.

Seizures

A seizure occurs due to disorganized and excessive electrical activity in the brain. Our brain cells communicate using coordinated electrical activity among cells. When this activity becomes disrupted, a seizure results. There are two broad categories of seizure, generalized and focal. Let's look at these in more detail.

Generalized seizures are caused by abnormal electrical activity in the entire brain. These seizures may cause convulsions in which the victim falls to the floor and has uncontrollable muscle movements. Victims may be unconscious during a generalized seizure.

In contrast, focal seizures affect only part of the brain. They cause more limited symptoms than generalized seizures, and the victim may be aware of the seizure occurring.

People with epilepsy may experience a particular sensation or feeling before the start of a seizure. Typical examples include an unusual smell or visual hallucination. This is known as an aura and indicates a seizure may be about to occur.

Although seizures can appear distressing, short seizures that resolve spontaneously are not normally life-threatening. However, prolonged seizures or seizures caused by another problem (for example, a head injury) *are* life-threatening and require urgent medical intervention to control the seizure and treat the underlying problem.

> **Medical Terminology**
>
> *Epilepsy* is a medical condition that causes recurrent seizures.

Be aware that some people with epilepsy wear alert bracelets or devices around their wrists, ankles, or necks to inform bystanders and medical staff that they have epilepsy. These may contain emergency contact information or instructions on what to do if the person experiences a seizure.

✚ Generalized Seizures

Here are some of the signs and symptoms of a major generalized seizure:

- Collapse and reduced level of consciousness
- Violent shaking episode (convulsion)
- Abnormal breathing
- Incontinence
- Tongue biting

+ First Aid Treatment for a Generalized Seizure

1. Remove any hazards from the area around the victim to make the scene safe.
2. Protect the victim's head.
3. Start timing the seizure.
4. Call EMS.
5. Once the jerking movements have stopped, open the victim's airway and place her in the recovery position (see Recovery Position in **PART 5**).
6. Do not attempt to restrain the victim or place anything in her mouth.
7. Provide reassurance and monitor vital signs until emergency medical help arrives.
8. Take steps to protect the victim's dignity (for example, ensure bystanders move on).

Some people with epilepsy will have occasional seizures and not require emergency medical help unless the seizure lasts for more than five minutes or they have multiple seizures or other complications. If you are unsure, always call EMS. Victims may be very tired following a seizure and want to sleep; this is normal as long as you're able to wake them up and they are not unconscious.

+ Common Seizure Myths

Unfortunately, there are many common myths circulating about the correct first aid treatment for someone having a major epileptic seizure. Never place anything into the mouth of someone having a seizure—this could cause blockage of her airway and result in serious harm. Never attempt to restrain a person having a seizure to stop the jerking movements. This is likely to cause harm to the victim or to you.

+ Focal Seizures

Some signs and symptoms of a focal seizure include:

- Jerking movements in arms or legs
- Repetitive actions such as lip smacking or swallowing
- Hallucinations

+ First Aid Treatment for a Focal Seizure

1. Remove any hazards from the area around the victim to make the scene safe.
2. Start timing the seizure.
3. Provide reassurance until the seizure resolves.
4. Advise the victim to seek medical attention.

Be aware that some focal seizures may progress to major generalized seizures.

Diabetic Hyperglycemia (High Blood Sugar)

Diabetes is a common medical condition that causes elevated blood sugar levels in the body. Diabetics often face particular challenges in emergency situations. Most of us know someone who is living with diabetes, as the condition is becoming much more common. There are two main types of diabetes: type 1 and type 2. If left untreated, both types will cause dangerously high blood sugar levels (hyperglycemia). This can lead to life-threatening complications including a diabetic coma. People living with diabetes are more at risk of heart attacks, strokes, and eye disease, especially if their blood sugar levels are persistently high. The main treatment for type 1 diabetes is the administration of insulin, via either regular injections or a continuous pump, with regular monitoring of blood sugar levels. If a diabetic person misses a dose of insulin, then she becomes at risk of developing high blood sugar levels. The basic treatment for type 2 diabetes is dietary changes. In some instances insulin treatment may be required as well.

These are some signs and symptoms of high blood sugar. If you have these symptoms, you should consult a medical professional immediately.

- Excessive thirst
- Frequent urination
- Weight loss
- Visual disturbances
- Reduced level of consciousness
- Headache
- Fatigue

Medical Terminology

Hyperglycemia is the medical term for high blood sugar.

✚ **First Aid Treatment for High Blood Sugar**
1. Call EMS.
2. If the victim becomes unconscious, open his airway and place him in the recovery position (see Recovery Position in **PART 5**).
3. Encourage the victim to record his own blood sugar reading and act upon this if able to do so.
4. Provide reassurance and monitor vital signs until emergency medical help arrives.
5. Don't attempt to administer insulin unless you are specifically trained and authorized to do so.

Diabetic Hypoglycemia (Low Blood Sugar)

Diabetes is a common medical condition that causes elevated blood sugar levels in the body. In the previous section, we looked at the symptoms and treatment of elevated blood sugar levels (hyperglycemia). In this section, we'll discuss what happens when blood sugar levels fall too low. Why might this happen? The main treatment for type 1 diabetes is the administration

Medical Terminology

Hypoglycemia is the term for low blood sugar.

of insulin, via either regular injections or a continuous pump, with regular monitoring of blood sugar levels. Type 2 diabetes may also be treated with insulin, often in combination with oral medications. People who administer insulin for diabetes (either type 1 or type 2) are at risk of developing low blood sugar levels. This can occur if too much insulin is administered or the person misses a meal after taking his or her insulin.

✚ Signs and Symptoms of Low Blood Sugar

- Changes in behavior (for example, irritability and aggression); these symptoms can mimic alcohol intoxication
- Confusion
- Sweating
- Headache
- Reduced level of consciousness
- Seizures
- Weakness or shakiness
- Fast or irregular heartbeat

✚ First Aid Treatment for Low Blood Sugar

1. If the person is conscious and able to swallow, give sugar by mouth using glucose tablets or a sugary drink.
2. Monitor the victim for ten to fifteen minutes; the symptoms should gradually resolve.
3. Encourage the person to test his own blood sugar levels if he is able to do so.
4. If the symptoms do not improve after ten to fifteen minutes after receiving glucose tablets or a sugary drink, or the person deteriorates, call EMS.

Testing Blood Sugar Levels

People with diabetes may carry a portable blood sugar monitoring kit. This allows them to check their blood sugar levels and can detect hyper- and hypoglycemia. If a member of your family is diabetic, be sure to put his or her blood sugar monitoring kit in your first aid kit.

Do not give sugar to a victim who is not fully conscious, or who is unable to swallow. There is a risk of the victim choking in this situation. Instead, immediately call EMS and be prepared to place the victim in the recovery position (see Recovery Position in **PART 5**).

Poisoning

Poisoning occurs when a person comes into contact with a harmful substance. Our homes contain many potential poisons that can be dangerous if they are swallowed (ingested) or come into contact with our skin or eyes. This possibility is greater during an emergency, when everyday life is disrupted. In the following sections, we will look at four common poisoning situations and their first aid treatments. Always seek medical advice when dealing with a poisoning situation. In the US, the American Association of Poison Control Centers help hotline (1-800-222-1222) provides free advice 24/7. If you are traveling abroad, other countries may have similar systems in place to provide advice regarding exposure to poisons.

Alcohol and Drugs

While many of us enjoy an alcoholic drink, excessive alcohol or recreational drug use can have a variety of harmful effects on the body. Acute alcohol or drug intoxication can be life-threatening. Unfortunately, every year more than two thousand Americans die from acute alcohol poisoning. Also, being intoxicated increases the risk of accidental death from other causes (for example, falling from a height or drowning), as alcohol interferes with our ability to make decisions and weigh risks. Alcohol intoxication can cause a victim to lose consciousness. This is a medical emergency like any other cause of unconsciousness. It is important not to brush off this situation as a victim being "just drunk." She may be at risk of blocking her airway. Also, be mindful that low blood sugar levels (see Diabetic Hypoglycemia earlier in this part) can mimic the symptoms of alcohol intoxication, so if the person is diabetic, medical help should be sought to check his blood sugar levels.

Opioid poisoning is becoming an increasing problem. Opioids are strong painkilling medications available by prescription. In addition, heroin is a common illegal opioid that is highly addictive. The CDC estimates that in 2018 opioids were involved in almost forty-seven thousand overdose deaths in the US. An overdose of opioid medication causes a victim to become unconscious and stop breathing, quickly leading to death if treatment isn't administered. The main treatment of opioid overdose is administration of the drug naloxone (a common brand name is Narcan). Naloxone reverses the effects of an opioid overdose and can be lifesaving in an emergency situation. There is increasing focus on training all emergency personnel in the use of naloxone, and in some communities, lay rescuers and opioid users are being trained in the use of this medicine. Naloxone can be administered using a nasal spray, meaning it can be used by rescuers with minimal training.

Signs and symptoms of alcohol or drug poisoning include:

- Vomiting
- Behavioral changes
- Confusion and aggression
- Reduced level of consciousness

✛ First Aid Treatment for Alcohol or Drug Poisoning

1. Call EMS immediately.
2. Ensure the scene is safe for you to approach; victims who are intoxicated may be unpredictable or aggressive.
3. If the victim appears unconscious, a sternal rub is recommended in a suspected overdose situation. If this does not work, try to stimulate him or her with pain by rubbing your knuckles into the sternum (the place in the middle of your chest where your ribs meet), or by rubbing your knuckles on their upper lip.

PART 7

Ensure her airway is open, and place her in the recovery position to reduce the risk of vomit blocking her airway (see Recovery Position in **PART 5**).

1. If the victim is conscious, ask what she has taken and how much.
2. Give medical professionals information on what has been ingested, and ensure the victim is not left alone.
3. If an opioid overdose is suspected, administer nasal naloxone if available.

Household Cleaning Products

Household cleaning products contain strong chemicals and substances that can cause significant harm. Cleaning products may be accidentally swallowed (for example, by a child attracted by the bright colors of the product). Alternatively, cleaning products can splash or spray onto the skin or into the eyes.

Here are some of the signs and symptoms of household cleaning product poisoning:

- Vomiting
- Abdominal pain
- Throat pain
- Burns
- Eye irritation
- Loss of vision
- Seizures
- Difficulty in breathing

+ First Aid Treatment for Household Cleaning Product Poisoning
1. Ensure the scene is safe for you to approach; do not expose yourself to the poison.

2. Try to determine what product the victim has come in contact with.
3. Call EMS if the victim appears unwell, collapses, has a seizure, is having trouble breathing, or is drowsy or unconscious.
4. Otherwise, contact your local poison control center for advice.
5. If the poison has contaminated the eye, wash the eye with running water for at least fifteen to twenty minutes.
6. If the poison has contaminated the skin, remove any affected clothing and wash the area with running water for at least twenty minutes.
7. Ensure any runoff water from eye or skin washing is directed away from you and the victim.

✦ Don't Induce Vomiting

Do not induce vomiting unless specifically advised to do so by a medical professional or your local poison control center. Inducing vomiting may cause further damage to the victim's digestive tract when the poison is brought back up.

Contacting Poison Control

In the US, you can contact the American Association of Poison Control Centers help hotline by calling 1-800-222-1222. The service is free and available twenty-four hours a day.

Carbon Monoxide

Carbon monoxide is a highly toxic gas generated by the incomplete burning of fuels such as coal, wood, and natural gas. Examples of situations that may generate carbon monoxide include campfires that haven't been put out properly and faulty boilers. During emergencies such as earthquakes, tornadoes, and hurricanes, home systems may spring leaks. The gas has no smell or taste, so it is very difficult to detect. Carbon monoxide poisoning is fatal, acts rapidly, and is responsible for about four hundred deaths a year in the US.

It can't be stressed enough that one of the best ways to avoid carbon monoxide poisoning is to install monitors throughout your home. If you don't have these monitors, these are some signs and symptoms of carbon monoxide poisoning:

- Headache
- Dizziness
- Vomiting
- Confusion
- Reduced level of consciousness

Protect Your Family with a Carbon Monoxide Alarm

Carbon monoxide gas is invisible and has no smell. This makes the gas deadly and difficult to detect. You can protect your family by investing in a carbon monoxide alarm at home, especially if you have an open fire or generator.

✚ First Aid Treatment for Carbon Monoxide Poisoning
1. Immediately call EMS and inform the 911 operator about the risk of carbon monoxide gas.
2. Do not enter a situation where you may put yourself at risk of carbon monoxide exposure.
3. If safe to do so, instruct the victim to move away from the potential source of carbon monoxide and into fresh air.
4. If the victim is unconscious and not breathing normally, update EMS and commence CPR if safe to do so (see How to Perform CPR in **PART 5**).
5. Provide reassurance and monitor vital signs until emergency medical help arrives.

PART 7

Food Poisoning

Food poisoning occurs when we eat food contaminated with harmful bacteria, viruses, or parasites. Many of us have experienced the unpleasant effects of food poisoning at some point in our lives. Common bacteria and viruses that cause food poisoning include norovirus, *E. coli*, and campylobacter. Incorrect storage or preparation of food (for example, undercooking meat or not refrigerating food) increases the risk of bacteria contaminating the food. Poor hand hygiene is another cause of contamination, as bacteria are easily transferred from our hands onto the food we touch. Unfortunately, there's no specific first aid treatment for food poisoning. Instead, you should try to prevent dehydration, and seek medical assistance if the symptoms are not subsiding. Knowing when to seek medical assistance is important; while most mild cases of food poisoning will not cause major problems, children, pregnant women, people with weakened immune systems or chronic health problems, and the elderly are at risk of developing complications from food poisoning. Unfortunately, every year there are a number of deaths in the US from severe food poisoning. Don't delay in seeking medical assistance if you are worried about a victim with food poisoning.

The signs and symptoms of food poisoning include:

- Diarrhea
- Nausea
- Vomiting
- Abdominal pain
- Loss of appetite
- High temperature (fever)

+ First Aid Treatment for Food Poisoning

1. Encourage oral fluids to prevent dehydration. Commercially available oral rehydration solutions (ORS), which replace essential salts and sugar, may be necessary; check with your doctor first.

2. Ensure you, the victim, and all household members perform adequate handwashing and strict cleaning habits in your living areas to reduce the risk of the infection spreading.
3. Seek medical help if you are concerned that the symptoms are not subsiding or the victim has other medical problems.

Young children, pregnant women, the elderly, and people with weakened immune systems or chronic health problems are most at risk from food poisoning. Severe cases of food poisoning can lead to dehydration and require hospital admission. Always seek help early if you are concerned about a victim with food poisoning.

Emergency Environmental Conditions

In emergency situations during either summer or winter, you should be aware of the warning signs of common environmental conditions such as heatstroke and hypothermia. Although not everyone's "normal" temperature is the same, the traditional standard thinking is that our bodies are designed to work effectively at a temperature range around 98.6°F (37°C). Being exposed to extreme weather can disrupt our ideal temperature and lead to overheating or hypothermia. Both of these conditions can be life-threatening if steps are not taken quickly to correct the temperature disturbance. In addition, you should be prepared to deal with other outdoor emergency situations such as lightning strikes, which are more common than you might think. In the next sections, we'll show you how to recognize and treat common conditions that you might encounter when exposed to the elements.

Hypothermia

Hypothermia occurs when a person's core body temperature drops to a dangerously low level. Hypothermia develops once the body temperature drops below 95°F (35°C). A temperature between 90°F (32.2°C) and 95°F (35°C) is considered mild hypothermia. A temperature between 82°F (27.7°C) and 90°F (32.2°C) is classed as moderate hypothermia, and a temperature below 82°F (27.7°C) is severe hypothermia, which is life-threatening if the victim does not receive emergency care. Young children, the elderly, and people who stay outdoors for long periods are most at risk for developing hypothermia. Other risk factors include alcohol and drug use, certain health conditions, and certain prescription medications. While hypothermia is commonly associated with being outside in colder weather, this condition can also develop when a victim is in a home with inadequate heating. Correct first aid treatment of hypothermia is important in order to raise the body temperature and prevent the victim from slipping into a coma. Unfortunately, there are a number of common myths regarding the correct way to treat a hypothermic victim; we discuss them later in the Common Hypothermia Myths list.

These are some signs and symptoms of hypothermia to watch for:

MILD TO MODERATE HYPOTHERMIA:
- Shivering
- Lack of coordination and loss of fine motor skills
- Confusion

SEVERE TO LIFE-THREATENING HYPOTHERMIA:
- Shivering stops
- Reduced level of consciousness
- Rigid muscles

+ First Aid Treatment for Hypothermia
1. If the victim is outside or exposed to the elements, move her to a warm, dry place if possible. If this is not possible, seek shelter.
2. Call EMS and the appropriate search and rescue team, if in a remote outdoor location.
3. Remove and replace any wet clothing.

PART 7

4. If the victim is conscious and able to swallow safely, give her warm noncaffeinated nonalcoholic drinks with sugar and high-energy food (for example, a chocolate bar, a cereal bar, or an energy bar).

5. Cover the victim in warm layers (for example, blankets) and ensure her head is covered. If possible, cover around her face loosely to prevent frostbite from developing on her ears or cheeks, but take care not to restrict the victim's breathing.

6. If available, place warm (not hot) wrapped hot-water bottles or reusable heat packs wrapped in cloth in the victim's armpits and groin.

7. If the victim becomes unconscious, she will need to be placed in the recovery position to protect the airway (see Recovery Position in **PART 5**).

8. Severe hypothermia can cause the heart to stop beating effectively. Be prepared to perform CPR if the victim stops breathing normally (see How to Perform CPR in **PART 5**).

Be aware of your own safety. If in an outdoor situation, take appropriate steps to ensure you do not develop hypothermia and become a second victim.

✦ Common Hypothermia Myths

There are a number of first aid myths regarding the correct treatment of hypothermia. These are addressed here:

- *Do not* rub alcohol on the victim's skin. Doing this will not warm her up; instead, it will draw blood away from the body's core and accelerate heat loss.
- *Do not* place the victim in a hot bath, as this will also draw blood away from the body's core. In addition, there is a risk of the victim sustaining a burn injury if she is placed in a tub of scalding hot water.
- *Do not* give the victim any drinks containing alcohol. Doing this will cause the blood vessels to dilate, and the body will lose more heat.

PART 7

Frostbite

If you, your friends, or your family is caught in an emergency situation in circumstances where heat sources are either minimal or nonexistent, you need to be aware of the risk of frostbite. Frostbite is caused by freezing of the skin and underlying tissue. The majority of cases of frostbite are preventable by wearing enough suitable warm clothing for the conditions. Toes, fingers, and the face are most at risk of developing frostbite, as these areas are farthest away from the body's core and therefore most at risk of freezing.

Frostbite is split into two main categories: superficial and deep. Superficial frostbite occurs when only the top layer of skin is frozen. This may cause blistering of the skin. Deep frostbite occurs when the underlying tissue is frozen. Deep frostbite can cause permanent damage to the skin and underlying muscle due to these structures freezing. There is a risk of infection, and the victim may require surgery to remove damaged tissue or, in severe cases, to amputate the affected limb.

These are some signs and symptoms of superficial frostbite:

- Numbness in the affected area
- Swelling
- Blistering of the skin

The early stages of frostbite can be easily missed because the initial symptoms are numbness and loss of sensation in the affected area.

Here are some of the signs and symptoms of deep frostbite:

- Blue-colored skin (will later be black-colored)
- Hard skin
- Formation of an ulcer

PART 7

+ First Aid Treatment for Frostbite

1. Seek medical assistance; rewarming a frostbite injury is very painful, and the victim may require strong painkillers and a thorough assessment of the frostbite injury.
2. Monitor the victim for the development of hypothermia (see Hypothermia earlier in this part), and move her to a warm, dry, sheltered place.
3. Remove any constricting items such as watches and rings near the affected area before the frostbitten area starts to swell.

If prompt medical assistance is not available:

1. Only consider rewarming if there is no risk of the affected area being refrozen.
2. To rewarm, place the affected area in warm (not hot) water at 99°F–104°F (around 37°C–40°C); the rewarming process takes about thirty minutes and is complete when the affected area has returned to a normal color and sensation is restored.
3. Protect the area by applying a sterile dressing and cover to prevent refreezing.

The rewarming process is very painful for the victim. If possible, seek medical assistance to ensure adequate pain relief can be given to keep the victim comfortable.

Heatstroke

In contrast to hypothermia (low body temperature), heatstroke is a life-threatening situation that occurs when the body becomes too hot and is unable to regulate temperature effectively. Heatstroke can be deadly, as the high body temperature causes vital organs to rapidly shut down. In addition, victims of heatstroke are often dehydrated, because excessive fluid is lost through sweating. A victim of heatstroke has a high risk of dying unless immediate steps are taken to reduce his body temperature and restore lost fluid. Active cooling is the main treatment in a heatstroke situation. All victims with suspected heatstroke need a thorough medical assessment, as they can develop complications affecting the heart, kidneys, and other vital organs. Children, the elderly, those with chronic health conditions, those on certain medications, and people with inadequate air-conditioning are most at risk of developing heatstroke, so you need to be vigilant, especially during periods of hot weather. Heatstroke can also be brought on by exercising in very hot conditions, and athletes or outdoor workers should be aware of the risk of heatstroke and know how to spot the warning signs in their peers.

Here are some of the signs and symptoms of heatstroke:

- Hot, red, dry, or damp skin
- Body temperature above 103°F (39.4°C)
- Reduced level of consciousness and confusion
- Increased pulse and respiratory rate
- Headache

✚ First Aid Treatment for Heatstroke

1. Immediately call EMS.
2. Move the victim to a cool and sheltered place.
3. Remove any excessive outer clothing.
4. Cool the victim by using cool cloths or a cool bath or by placing ice packs in his groin, neck, back, and armpits.
5. If the victim becomes unconscious, he will need to be placed in the recovery position to protect the airway (see Recovery Position in **PART 5**).
6. Be prepared to perform CPR if the victim loses consciousness and stops breathing normally (see How to Perform CPR in **PART 5**).

Take care not to overcool the victim and cause hypothermia.

Sunburn

During some emergency situations, overexposure to the sun can be common. We've probably all experienced sunburn at some point. But how many of us actually perform simple first aid measures to help our skin recover properly from the burn? Sunburn is caused by exposure to ultraviolet (UV) radiation from the sun, which damages the superficial skin tissue. Sunburn is painful but often heals with no significant complications. However, prolonged exposure to UV radiation increases the risk of skin cancer and accelerates the aging process in the skin. Severe sunburn can occasionally cause significant burns that require specialist medical intervention. Prevention is always better than cure when considering sunburn; protect yourself and your family by taking appropriate steps to reduce sun exposure (see Protecting Yourself from Sunburn in this part). Most sunburn can be treated at home with self-care measures. However, severe cases will require a medical assessment, especially if there are large blisters.

✦ Protecting Yourself from Sunburn
- Apply sunscreen with a high SPF liberally over all areas of exposed skin at least twenty minutes before sun exposure.
- Reapply sunscreen at least every two hours or after any immersion in water or strenuous activity.
- Wear appropriate clothing and cover exposed areas.
- Avoid being in the sun during the hottest part of the day (10 a.m.–4 p.m.).

These are some signs and symptoms of sunburn:

- A history of exposure to direct sunlight
- Pink or red, painful skin
- Peeling or blistering of the skin
- Itching

+ **First Aid Treatment for Sunburn**
  1. Avoid further exposure to the sun.
  2. Cool the skin with cool baths or cloths.
  3. Apply after-sun lotion.
  4. Encourage sips of water to prevent dehydration.
  5. Do not burst any blisters that form. If a blister bursts on its own, gently clean the area to prevent infection and apply a sterile dressing. If the wound left by the burst blister is showing signs of infection, seek medical attention as soon as possible.

+ **Burn Injury Myths**

There are many myths regarding the correct treatment of burns. Like other types of burns, sunburns should be cooled only with cool water to remove heat from the burn.

- Do not apply toothpaste or butter to a burn. This will not cool the burn adequately and can introduce infection. The best method to cool down a minor burn is with cool water.
- Do not burst blisters, as this will increase the risk of infection in the burn.
- Do not place ice on a minor burn to speed up the cooling process. This could cause freeze burns to the skin.

Lightning Strike

Being struck by lightning is not as rare as you might think. More than twenty people in the US are killed each year by being hit by lightning. Many more victims are struck by lightning and survive. Statistics show only around 10 percent of lightning strikes are fatal. Lightning strikes can cause severe electrical burns and disrupt the electrical activity of the heart, causing a cardiac arrest. The victim may be thrown to the ground and sustain further injuries including head injuries or limb fractures. If you find yourself caught outside in a thunderstorm, seek shelter immediately in a building or hardtop vehicle with the windows up, and stay there for at least thirty minutes after the storm has completely passed. If you can't find shelter quickly, avoid high ground, and stay away from tall objects, open spaces, and water. Many people believe that crouching down is an effective way to stay safe during a thunderstorm; however, you are still at risk if you remain outdoors. Seeking shelter is the only effective way to protect yourself from a lightning strike. If no other shelter is available, a car will provide some limited protection from a lightning strike, although this isn't due to the rubber in the tires as most people believe. The metal body of a car will conduct the electricity from a lightning strike to the ground. Obviously, this only works when the car has a metal shell—unfortunately, a soft-top convertible will not keep you safe during a thunderstorm. Stay away from landline phones and plumbing fixtures. Lighting strikes can be transmitted via both.

+ First Aid Treatment for a Lightning Strike

1. Consider your own safety, and take immediate shelter indoors if there is a risk of further lightning strikes.
2. Immediately call EMS.
3. The victim is safe to touch after a lightning strike; the body will not retain any electrical charge.
4. If the victim is conscious, assess for any injuries and burns. Monitor vital signs and provide reassurance until medical help arrives. Move the victim to shelter if safe to do so.
5. If the victim is unconscious, assess for the presence of normal breathing and commence CPR if required (see How to Perform CPR in **PART 5**).

Near-Drowning

In the event of floods or other emergencies, near-drowning may occur, sometimes on a large scale. Witnessing a near-drowning incident is terrifying. If a victim is successfully rescued from the water, there is inevitably much relief among bystanders and rescuers. However, most people don't realize that the victim is still at risk of serious medical complications. This is where you can help save her life. She may be out of the water, but she's not out of danger.

A victim may appear to have recovered from being in the water then suddenly deteriorate and become unwell. Why does this occur? First, the victim may develop hypothermia (dangerously low body temperature), especially if the water is very cold. Wet clothing causes a significant amount of heat loss and puts the victim at risk of hypothermia. If water has entered the victim's throat, there is a risk of the voice box going into spasm. This is a serious situation, since the spasm causes the victim's airway to close up, and air can't enter the lungs. Advanced medical help is urgently required to protect the airway and stop the victim from suffocating.

If water has entered the victim's lungs, the water can irritate the lungs and cause breathing problems. This situation is known as secondary drowning and can sometimes take up to seventy-two hours to develop after a near-drowning situation.

Always seek medical attention if a victim has been rescued from a near-drowning situation. There's not much you can do in first aid to fix the underlying problem of near-drowning; these victims need urgent specialist medical help to protect their airway and stop further lung damage.

Here are some of the signs and symptoms of near-drowning:

- Difficulty in breathing
- Increased respiratory rate
- Coughing
- Chest pain
- Vomiting
- Pale, cold skin

PART 7

+ First Aid Treatment for Near-Drowning

1. Immediately call EMS.

2. Provide reassurance and monitor vital signs until emergency medical help arrives.

3. Remove any wet clothing and monitor the victim closely for the development of hypothermia (see Hypothermia earlier in this part).

4. If the victim loses consciousness, assess whether she is breathing normally. If she is not breathing normally, immediately update EMS and commence CPR until the arrival of medical help (see How to Perform CPR in **PART 5**).

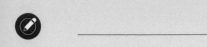

AFTERWORD

You won't always be able to determine exactly when the next hurricane will hit, whether a tornado will sweep through your town, or when the country will be threatened by another pandemic, but with *In Case of Emergency: The Family Disaster Organizer*, you'll know that you and your family will be ready for the challenges you'll face if disaster or disease strikes. You've already taken the most important step toward preparedness by reading this book and recording your family's financial and medical information. In doing so, you have provided yourself with the ultimate tool for making it through an unexpected emergency, because everything you will need to know—from what supplies you should have and what medications you'll need to take, to instructions on how to make a sling and the correct treatment for an open fracture—will always be within arm's reach. You'll also have easy access to details about the life you may need to temporarily leave behind, because the pocket of this book will be full of the items and documents (like spare keys and copies of property deeds) that are important to you and your family.

Functioning as one of the most important tools in your seventy-two-hour kit, *In Case of Emergency: The Family Disaster Organizer* will give you the confidence and security you'll need to help your family survive and recover from even the most devastating situations.

APPENDIX

First Aid Techniques

Handwashing to Protect Yourself from Infection

Performing proper handwashing is one of the most effective ways to stop the spread of contagious diseases such as the common cold, influenza, and stomach viruses. You should aim to perform handwashing at regular intervals to reduce the risk of infection to yourself and the victim. For handwashing to be effective, it needs to be performed thoroughly. Let's take a look at how to properly clean your hands.

First, the most effective way to wash your hands is with running water and soap. Hand sanitizer gels are less effective, especially if your hands are visibly dirty. However, if you have no access to running water, then using hand sanitizer gel is much better than not cleaning your hands at all. The CDC recommends using an alcohol hand sanitizer gel with a minimum concentration of 60 percent alcohol to provide effective protection against germs.

Effective handwashing should take at least forty seconds to a minute, with the scrubbing part taking a minimum of twenty seconds to complete. This time is required to effectively remove all the germs and dirt from your hands. Quickly rinsing your hands underneath a tap is unlikely to remove germs from your hands and will not protect you from catching or passing on a dangerous infection. So don't rush handwashing!

Towels Carry Germs

Believe it or not, reusable towels in our homes can easily become contaminated with dangerous bacteria. Damp towels are a perfect breeding ground for germs, and research has shown these towels are often responsible for transmitting germs and infection. Disposable hand towels should ideally be used whenever you are washing your hands to reduce the risk of your clean hands becoming contaminated.

HOW TO PERFORM EFFECTIVE HANDWASHING:

1. Turn on the tap and adjust the water to a warm, comfortable temperature; wet your hands and apply enough soap to cover all surfaces of your hands.

2. Rub the palms of your hands together to lather the soap.
3. Rub the top of your left hand with your right hand, and interlace the fingers; then switch to the other hand.
4. Rub your hands palm to palm with your fingers interlaced.
5. Rub the backs of your fingers against the opposing palm, then switch; rub the backs of your hands together.
6. Hold your right thumb in your left fist and rotate, then switch.
7. Rub your nails/the tips of your fingers against the opposite palm (this cleans under your nails), then switch.
8. Place your right hand over your left wrist and scrub by twisting your hand, then switch.
9. After scrubbing your hands for at least twenty seconds, rinse.
10. Dry hands thoroughly with a disposable towel (see previous sidebar, Towels Carry Germs).
11. Use the towel to turn off the faucet.

Your hands are now clean.

Applying a Pressure Bandage to Stop Bleeding

A pressure bandage is used to cover a major wound and stop the bleeding. The bandage has two parts. First, a sterile pad, which is placed over the wound to cover it. Second, the elastic tail of the bandage attached to the sterile pad, which is used to wrap around the injury and apply pressure over the wound. All first aid kits should contain pressure bandages to enable you to treat wounds effectively. Because pressure bandages are sterile (free from germs), they will have an expiration date printed on the package. After this date, the bandage may no longer be completely sterile, and could introduce infection into the wound.

HOW TO APPLY A PRESSURE BANDAGE:
1. Choose a pressure bandage large enough to cover the entire wound; check that the bandage is up-to-date.

2. Ensure you are wearing disposable gloves to protect you from the victim's blood.
3. Open the sterile packaging of the bandage, taking care not to touch the sterile pad, as this could risk introducing infection.
4. Place the sterile pad directly over the wound and apply firm pressure.
5. Wrap the long tail of the bandage firmly around the sterile pad to keep pressure applied over the wound.
6. Continue wrapping the long tail around the sterile pad, ensuring the edges of the pad are covered.
7. Tie the two ends of the bandage over the wound.

Making a Sling for a Broken Arm

Most first aid kits contain triangular-shaped bandages to make arm slings. If an arm is broken, a sling can help by reducing movement until the victim can seek medical assistance.

HOW TO MAKE A SLING:
1. Place the triangular bandage underneath the injured arm with the middle point of the triangle sitting beneath the victim's elbow (think "point to the joint" to remember this).
2. Place the top end of the triangular bandage over the victim's opposite shoulder and around the back of the neck.
3. Bring the bottom end of the sling up over the forearm and tie the two ends together at the side of the victim's neck.
4. Ensure the sling is fully supporting the elbow and wrist.
5. Secure the point of the triangle with tape or a safety pin. If a triangular bandage is not available, you can improvise a sling with a scarf or a coat. As long as the arm is supported, it doesn't matter what material is used to make the sling.

Strapping a Sprained Ankle to Provide Support

Sprains and strains to the ankle can be managed by using the PRICE first aid treatment (see First Aid Treatment for a Soft-Tissue Injury in PART 5). Bandaging an injured ankle can provide support to the joint and reduce inflammation and swelling. Most first aid kits contain elastic bandages for use in this situation. You can also buy specialized ankle supports; however, these are not normally available in most first aid kits. If you are going to strap a sprained ankle, you need to be careful not to apply the bandage so tightly as to constrict blood supply to the foot. The bandage should provide comfortable support to the joint but not be so tight as to cut off blood flow to the area beyond the bandage.

There are many different methods to strap an ankle. The following is one of the most common methods used.

HOW TO STRAP AN ANKLE:
1. Open up the elastic bandage.
2. Start at the toes, where they join the rest of the foot; tips of the toes are left unwrapped.
3. Start bandaging the foot by wrapping the bandage several times around the body of the foot.
4. Each new wrap of the bandage should overlap the previous wrap by approximately half as you work your way up the foot.
5. At the ankle, wrap the bandage in a figure-eight around the back of the ankle.
6. After strapping the ankle itself, work up the calf a couple of inches past the ankle to provide additional support.
7. Secure the bandage in place. The bandage needs to be applied firmly to provide support but shouldn't be so tight as to constrict blood flow to the limb.

Seek Medical Attention If You Suspect a Fracture

Telling the difference between a badly sprained ankle and a fractured one is very difficult, even for a medical professional! Often, an X-ray is required to check for a fracture in the ankle. Always seek medical attention if you are concerned that the victim may have fractured her ankle.

Irrigating an Eye to Remove a Foreign Body

You'll need to act quickly if a victim has sustained a foreign body in his eye. Irrigation can remove the object if it is superficial. Never attempt to remove an object that is embedded in the eye. (See Foreign Body in the Eye in **PART 5** for more information on treating a victim with a foreign body in his eye.) You'll always need to seek professional advice from a doctor or eye specialist to ensure no permanent damage has been caused to the eye. The tissues of the eye are very delicate, and even a small foreign body, such as a piece of grit or metal, can scratch the surface of the eye.

HOW TO IRRIGATE AN EYE:
1. Sit the victim down, and ask him to face the light.
2. Wash your hands with soap and running water.
3. Put on disposable gloves.
4. Inspect the eye to find the foreign object. Only attempt to remove superficial small objects with irrigation.
5. Tilt the head backward and to the side of the affected eye; place a towel (if available) to cover the victim's clothing on the affected side.
6. Pour a gentle stream of clean water or sterile eyewash solution into the inner corner of his eye; you are aiming to wash away the object from the surface of the eye.
7. Reinspect the eye to see if the object has been removed.
8. Seek professional medical advice.

Bandaging a Blister

Blisters can be bandaged to protect the area from further damage and to reduce the risk of infection. Remember, it is not advised to burst blisters since this can increase the risk of infection. (See Blisters in **PART 5** for more information on the correct first aid for a victim with a blister.)

BANDAGE A BLISTER:

1. Wash your hands with soap and running water.
2. Apply disposable gloves.
3. If the blister is small, apply a regular bandage or specialized blister bandage to cover the area; make sure to check that the padded area of the bandage is large enough to cover the entire blister without any of the adhesive material sticking to the blister.
4. If the blister is large, cover with a piece of gauze and secure in place loosely with a bandage.

INDEX

About the Author

Allison Stewart, MPH, is a trained epidemiologist with hands-on experience with disaster response, including outbreak response. At her previous position at the Houston Health Department, she was in charge of surveillance at the shelters following Hurricane Ike and was significantly involved in the H1N1 pandemic outbreak response. Allison was also recruited for disaster response for the Ebola outbreak in West Africa in 2014 and spent five months working at the Ebola Treatment Center. Allison is currently employed as an epidemiologist as part of the COVID-19 pandemic response.